THE ART OF TRAINING PLANTS

*the text of this book is printed
on 100% recycled paper*

FIG. 1. *Gardenia jasminoides*. Pruning is the key to success in growing a decorative gardenia.

THE art OF TRAINING plants

ERNESTA DRINKER BALLARD

BARNES & NOBLE BOOKS

A DIVISION OF HARPER & ROW, PUBLISHERS

New York, Evanston, San Francisco, London

This book represents to a large degree a joint effort with my husband, Frederic L. Ballard, Jr. Many of the plants pictured were shaped and planted by him, and many of the ideas set forth have grown out of our observations and discussions together. In addition, he has been untiring in helping to make the text accurate and readable.

E.D.B.

CONTENTS

INTRODUCTION

With each year I spend gardening indoors and on my terrace, I take increased pleasure in individual plants—in watching a dwarfed tree develop into a miniature replica of its natural brothers, or the slow growth of a bromeliad along a weathered piece of cedar, or the graceful cascade of a trailing plant from a hanging basket. Paying attention to particular plants over months or years, I have become aware of their aesthetic qualities, and I have attempted to combine horticultural skill with creative instincts to make each a decoration that can be used on a table or mantel, or in a corner or entryway, like a piece of sculpture. Figure 1 shows the kind of plant I have in mind.

This book is about such decorative plants. It tells what I have learned about planting, pruning, and training specimens, not only to make, but to keep them beautiful. I emphasize the idea of keeping them beautiful because no plant is permanent. All grow and branch, lose leaves, and develop new ones. Their size, shape, balance, and proportions change, necessitating constant attention to keep them ornamental.

Some of my decorative plants are the hardy trees and woody shrubs associated with oriental bonsai; others are tropical species more suited to indoor growing; still others are the soft-stemmed herbaceous plants (begonias, geraniums, and such), or the cacti and succulents, used for generations as house plants. All have two things that set them apart from mass-produced products. First, they are individually trained and pruned to aesthetically satisfying shapes. Second, they are planted in containers chosen to match their shapes, colors, and textures.

A plant carefully grown and properly planted may almost be said to have a personality. Its health reflects the daily care expended on it, and it intrigues its grower over and over again with subtle changes in balance and design resulting from its own growth and the frequent trimming that is essential to this kind of horticulture.

Dr. John M. Fogg, director of the Morris Arboretum of the University of Pennsylvania, tells a story that illustrates my point. On a trip to India he visited a sculptor who had two prize trees growing in his garden. They were tamarinds (*Tamarindus indica*), a widely grown native species, and were virtually identical in every respect but size. One was planted in the earth and was forty feet high; the other grew in a pot and was three feet high. The sculptor told Dr. Fogg that in thirty years not a single day had passed in which he had not attended in some way to his little tree—pruning, trimming, or bending. The result was a replica of the mature tree with all the charm that miniatures exert in any field of art.

This book will not set out the basic botanical principles and horticultural techniques of indoor gardening. I have written about them in *Garden in Your House*. Rather, I will here suggest to pot gardeners, indoors and out, how they can apply these principles and use these techniques to create objects of art from living plants.

My ideas about decorative plants trace back to Japanese bonsai. I shall never forget the first one I saw—a five-needle pine, perhaps fifty years old and about fifteen inches high, planted on a mossy mound in a shallow dish, the mound stretching away from the trunk like a tiny meadow. It gave me a glimpse of a different kind of horticulture, one in which the emphasis is on stability, maturity, and perfection of detail, as contrasted with the culture of large-leaved tropical foliage plants, in which the emphasis is on rapid growth and often on sheer size.

But whereas the classical practice of bonsai was limited, first by the lack of heat and later by tradition, to plant material hardy in China and Japan; I have found that there is virtually no end to the variety of plants that can be grown to attractive specimens in modern houses, sunporches, and greenhouses. Indeed, the traditional hardy bonsai material, which needs near-freezing temperatures during the dormant season, yet cannot stand prolonged frost, is harder for Americans to manage than many exotic species. The resourceful pot gardener will find situations in and around his house for plants from every part of the world: warm, humid places for jungle dwellers; cool, sunny places for subtropical species; and cold, protected corners where the potted trees and shrubs of the temperate zones can spend a dormant winter. And so this book includes discussions and pictures of decorative plants from all over the world.

In selecting these pictures I have resisted the temptation to concentrate on breath-taking specimens. All the plants illustrated here except the bonsai in Figures 3, 4 and 8 were grown in this country and were trained within the last four years. Those in Figures 22, 31, 33 and 36 belong to friends; the rest are in my own collection.

The pictures show what can be achieved by an American gardener in a relatively short time. However, I would be less than candid if I did not warn the reader that considerable skill and experience, and a great deal of devotion, are required to produce results such as these. Like any potted plant they need regular watering, fertilizing and insect control, and periodic repotting. In addition the woody species usually need to be shaped by wiring, bracing or staying, and all decorative plants need pinching, pruning and grooming almost every day.

In preparing the pictures I have tried to present the plants as they are and to avoid the effects which sometimes make a photograph look better than the original. In most cases the plants are shown against neutral backgrounds to bring out as much detail as possible. I rely on my reader's imagination to picture them on his own piano (as in Fig. 19) or mantel piece (as in Fig. 13) or as a centerpiece at dinner. Decorative plants, like any others, must be grown in a place with adequate light, heat and humidity, but they can be temporarily displayed wherever an ornament is desired.

In techniques as well as in material, I have drawn on current Japanese practices but have tried to develop and explain them for today's gardeners. I shall show that for the most part the methods used by the Japanese in shaping plants and keeping them small are not oriental mysteries but simply applications of familiar horticultural principles. And I shall also try to show how to use these methods to produce handsome, pleasing results. I shall cover pruning (both roots and branches), wiring, bending, and potting, and shall suggest some plant material and suitable containers. And I shall also suggest places for growing bonsai when they are not on display.

It is my hope that readers of this book will no longer be satisfied with standardized dish gardens and philodendrons growing on totem poles, but will want to create decorative plants of their own in styles suited to their own houses and tastes. Those who do will find that they have added to the usual pleasure of growing plants the satisfaction of learning and using new technical skills and the joy of artistic creation.

ONE

SOME DECORATIVE PLANTS

TRADITIONAL BONSAI

Good bonsai are the epitome of decorative plants, the finest combination of horticultural skill and artistic taste. While growing traditional bonsai is impractical for many Americans, familiarity with bonsai history and methods is a valuable foundation for anyone who wants to achieve beauty and distinction in potted plants.

History of bonsai

Bonsai is a Japanese word composed of characters meaning "tray" or "pot" and "to plant." It can be loosely translated to mean a small tree or trees in a pot. Apparently, the Japanese themselves derived the word from the Chinese P'an-tsai, meaning "table culture"—which has been described by Dr. H. L. Li in his book Chinese Flower Arrangement (Philadelphia: Hedera House, 1956):

> Table culture represents the culmination of garden art of China, the reproduction of idealized landscapes in reduced scale. Because of the extreme limitation of space, only one or a few plants can be grown in one culture. The plants are often the central feature of interest, while the landscape effect is usually reduced to a single piece of stone, and sometimes the judicious use of mosses or weeds for a background or screening the soil.
>
> For the untrained eye, miniature trees often appear grotesque or awkward. They, however, actually represent certain natural features that are much accentuated in Chinese art. The traditional landscapes in Chinese painting, the characteristic precipitous rocky peaks with gnarled pines, are realistic portrayals of some of the scenic mountains in China. Thus, the shapes assumed by most miniature trees are na-

tural, though uncommon, forms that convey best the artistic features in the Chinese sense. The love of ancient dwarf trees in China is also a manifestation of the great veneration regarding everything that is old.

Dr. Li tells us that table culture was well established in China by the tenth century. In Japan, bonsai appear in picture scrolls as early as the thirteenth century, and there is a famous fifteenth century Japanese play, called *The Potted Trees,* in which a poor samurai burns his cherished bonsai to warm a stranger who happily turns out to be the emperor.

In those early times, bonsai appear to have had only limited popularity. It was not until the middle of the nineteenth century that the collection and culture of miniature trees became a Japanese national fad. Today, the Japanese bonsai fancier trains and grows the trees himself, trades them with others, buys them from professional growers, visits bonsai exhibitions, and displays his best trees in bonsai shows, very much as an amateur painter in America enjoys the pleasures of his own creations and admires the creations of experts.

Care of hardy bonsai

As a result of recent wars, the improvement in trans-Pacific air travel, and the revival of trade with Japan, an increasing number of Americans have become interested in the Orient, and particularly in oriental furnishings and decoration. An outgrowth of this interest is the desire to own bonsai, a desire that as often as not arises in persons who have no background in horticulture. The results are not always happy.

Growing bonsai, even in Japan, is a delicate and demanding art. In this country it is even more difficult. The plants traditionally used are hardy species, native to China and Japan—pines, spruces, maples, cherries, and the like. They are used to a relatively mild climate where dew, fog and frequent light rains keep them from drying out. Sitting on a terrace or patio in our hot, dry summers and autumns, they must be watered every day when it is not foggy or rainy, and twice or even three times a day when it is hot, dry, and windy. Someone sensitive to their needs must check the plants each day in the forenoon and again in the afternoon and water them if they are dry. One omission on a hot, dry day will kill half of them. Two will probably kill them all.

For people living in the northern half of the United States, winter care presents equally difficult problems. Hardy bonsai cannot be treated like house plants. They will not tolerate conditions in which philodendrons and begonias thrive. The heated air of our houses, even when humidified by evaporation from wet pebbles, is far too dry for plants like these.

On the other hand, they cannot be exposed to the full rigors of winter. Indeed, many species native to China and Japan are not hardy north of a line running roughly from Boston through St. Louis to central New Mexico and thence to Vancouver. While freezing temperatures, as such, will not harm them, the combination of prolonged frost and dry winter winds will often dry them out and kill them. The reason for this is that freezing causes the water in the upper layers of the soil to coagulate into frost crystals, stripping the roots of their usual layer of moisture and forming cavities in the earth through which the winter air circulates. This dry air draws moisture from the roots with the same desiccating effect as if the plant had been left bare-rooted on a summer day. Desiccation threatens any shallow-rooted plant in winter. The threat is greater with bonsai because of their excessively small root systems. Incidentally, soaking the root ball is not the answer, since a thoroughly wet mass of soil will expand when it freezes and crack the pot.

What, then, are the best conditions for wintering bonsai? I would recommend a place sheltered from the wind where the temperature never goes below 28°. While it is possible to keep hardy bonsai growing all winter in a 55° greenhouse, and perhaps on a cool porch or window sill, I have much better results when I subject them to night temperatures well below 40° for six weeks or two months, inducing complete dormancy. Such a period of rest is a prerequisite for the burst of bloom and fresh foliage that we

Roche

FIG. 2. My bonsai house. The roof and sides will be closed in from November to April with removable plastic panels. Evergreens, which need more sun in winter, are on the top shelf. Deciduous trees are underneath.

associate with spring. Plants that are never dormant have no well-defined spring. They tend to form buds and new growth on different branches at different times throughout the year and, in my experience, do not grow satisfactorily.

My personal solution to wintering bonsai is a greenhouse designed to use commercial preglazed plastic panels. In the fall we install the panels in the roof and sides and plug in an electric heater with a low-temperature thermostat set to call for heat at 35° F. During the extraordinarily cold winter of 1960–1961, the interior temperature occasionally dropped to 28° F. at night, freezing the root balls of the plants nearest the walls; but in most cases the roots thawed during the day. Watering was required about every other day in sunny weather and perhaps every fourth or fifth day when the sky was cloudy or the house was covered with snow. In the early spring, a good six weeks before blossoms appeared outside, my bonsai crabapples and azaleas came into full bloom.

When all danger of frost is past, I remove the plastic panels, converting the greenhouse into an open framework with bonsai on the benches and fuchsias and lantanas hanging from the roof bars. It makes a pleasant summerhouse—one that I frequently find myself sharing with hummingbirds, who particularly relish these two species.

Before we built our plastic shelter (Fig. 2), we wintered our hardy bonsai in standard cold frames and in ground beds protected from the wind. To minimize the danger of their drying out, we sank the plants in the ground so that the tops of their root balls were about a half inch below the surface. The first winter we dug them in without removing their containers, many of which cracked in the frost. Thereafter we took the plants out of their pots and dug their exposed root balls into the ground. Since there is little or no root growth in the dormant season, we had no difficulty in putting them back into the same pots in the early spring.

Of course, there are many other kinds of place for hardy bonsai in the winter, some of which I will describe in the pages that follow. The important point is that winter care is in many ways as demanding as summer care and, like summer care, requires a knowledge of horticulture and a sensitivity to the needs of the plants.

Traditional, hardy bonsai are decorative, but they cannot be treated merely as decorations. Their care is exacting. A person desiring to grow them and lacking horticultural experience should start with the tropical bonsai described later in this chapter. They are cheaper to buy and easier to grow. When you can keep that kind of plant alive and decorative, it will be time enough to invest in hardy bonsai.

Enjoying hardy bonsai

The way to enjoy any decorative plant is to have it where it will strike your eye in moments of relaxation—at mealtime, or coffee time, or with a cooling drink in the long summer evenings. Bonsai look best when they are elevated nearly to eye level, so that you can see the trunk and roots as well as the foliage.

During the warm months from April 1 through November 15, this presents no problem. Bonsai, whether hardy or tropical, can be set on the wall of a terrace (Fig. 34) or patio or on a stump or rock in a garden. If you have a large collection, you may find it convenient to build tables with slats or gratings that will hold the plants at the desired height and let light and water through to the grass beneath (Fig. 2). You can set the plants in high, filtered shade or in direct sun. But you will find that several hours of unbroken sunlight makes watering critical, which is probably why California growers uniformly recommend shade. On the other hand, avoid constant heavy shade; the plants need light to live.

In winter the display of hardy bonsai is more difficult. Dormant plants will begin to resume growth if they are kept in a warm place more than a few days. And once growth has started, they cannot safely be exposed to near freezing temperatures again. So if you do bring them into the house for a party in wintertime, put them back in a cold spot the next day.

One of the most satisfactory solutions to the problem I have seen is a cool glassed-in entrance where the plants can stay all winter. They catch one's eye on entering or leaving the house, and can be glimpsed through the windows of the living room.

Imported bonsai

The tree in Figure 3 is *Pinus parviflora,* the Japanese white pine, commonly called five-needle pine. Because of its dense foliage

Brooklyn Botanic Garden

FIG. 3. Five-needle pine, *Pinus parviflora,* in the Holsten collection at the Brooklyn Botanic Garden.

and spreading growth habit, it lends itself to dwarfing and in Japan is a favorite for bonsai work. The plant pictured is between thirty and forty years old, has been grown on the stone slab for twelve years, and represents bonsai at its best. It needs full sunlight in winter and sun for either all or most of the day in summer, since adequate light is essential to satisfactory growth in pines. The crucial factor with such full foliage and so little soil is water. On hot, dry days the plant will transpire freely, and there will also be abundant evaporation from the exposed surface of the soil. Two or three waterings will be required.

This specimen grows in the Brooklyn Botanic Garden and was imported from Japan in 1960. It is part of an extensive collection at the Garden, which has been a pioneer in the East in collecting bonsai and in giving courses in bonsai techniques.

Most of the hardy dwarf trees at the Brooklyn Botanic Garden are wintered in a specially designed, deep cold frame. The plants sit on an eight-inch layer of washed pebbles, the top surface of which is two feet below ground level. The sides of the frame, which extend a foot or two above the ground, are of thick boards insulated on the inside. The sash, instead of being glazed, is covered with two thicknesses of polyethylene film, one above and one below the wooden sash frames, so that there is an insulating layer of air between them. The specimen in the picture, because it is so susceptible to drying out, will be wintered in the greenhouse at a temperature between 40° F. and 50° F. This is cool enough to induce dormancy but not so cold as to incur the risk of freezing.

Figure 4 shows two truly venerable bonsai, both *Chamaecyparis obtusa,* more than 150 years old. (If you have been sold a bonsai and told it was over a hundred years old, you have probably been fooled. Any plant of such great age is a collector's item and far beyond the average gardener's price range.) This tree is part of a collection which was imported in 1912 by Larz Anderson, then ambassador to Japan. The collection was given to the Arnold Arboretum of Harvard University by Mrs. Anderson in memory of the friendship between her husband and Charles Sargent, first director of the Arboretum. It is even more remarkable today than it was when first imported fifty years ago. Old trees such as this become widely known and appreciated like masterpieces in any art. They really should be accompanied by a log, telling, in the words of Yuji Yoshimura, "their history, who owned, and who enjoyed."

The Arnold Arboretum collection spends the summer in a lath house affording partial shade from summer sun. Even so, the plants must be checked daily to see if their roots are dry. They winter in an unheated pit house whose floor is seven feet below the ground level. Here the trees are protected from frost and direct sun and need watering about once a week.

FIG. 4. Two truly venerable bonsai, *Chamaecyparis obtusa*, both over 150 years old, from the Larz Anderson collection at the Arnold Arboretum.

Importing procedures

It is temping to import a plant like those in Figures 3 and 4, but before doing so you should be aware of the problems and risks.

In order to bring any plant material into this country, you must get an import permit from the United States Department of Agriculture. No permit can be obtained for certain species, including fir, maple, bamboo, citrus, apple, spruce, apricot, cherry, plum, peach, pear, and oak. For certain other species, such as euonymus, ash, holly, jasmine, juniper, rose, elm, and wisteria, permits are conditioned on a post-entry quarantine which most amateurs would not be qualified to carry out. For other species, permits are issued as a matter of course.

All material permitted entry must clear quarantine at the inspection station nearest to the port of arrival, the most likely stations for clearance being Honolulu, Seattle, San Francisco, San Pedro, and New York.

Plants for import must be free of soil before shipment; only moistened peat moss, sphagnum, coconut fiber, or damp newspaper may be packed around the roots. If a deciduous tree like the zelkova in Figure 8 is subjected to this treatment in the dormant season and is packed and shipped with care and speed, the chances of survival are somewhat better than even. Not so with evergreens. Because they never lose all their leaves and are therefore constantly losing moisture, their survival rate is not more than 20 per cent. In any case, air shipments are safest because the time involved is so much less.

Also, the plants must be appropriately labeled, preferably with the scientific name. This enables the inspectors to determine the procedure to be carried out at the quarantine station, where all plants are subject to fumigation or other treatment to avoid introducing pests like the Japanese beetle or the oriental fruit moth.

Detailed information on bonsai importation can be obtained from the United States Department of Agriculture, Permit Section, 209 River Street, Hoboken, New Jersey.

Natural bonsai

By natural bonsai I mean plants whose basic shapes are formed by the elements in their native sites before they are collected and potted. These naturally shaped trees are highly prized in Japan, and collectors have been so assiduous in seeking them out that there are said to be few left in that country.

The collection of natural bonsai can be a vacation in itself. It entails journeying to places where plants are naturally dwarfed— the mountains, the seashore, or a rocky cliff—searching out suitable specimens, digging them up with as much root as possible, and growing them with great care until new roots are formed. A bonsai-collecting expedition combines the pleasures of a walk in the country with the satisfaction of having something of value to show for the day's effort. After a few trips of this kind, you will find that you know a great deal more about rocks, moss, trunks, and roots, and how they look when trees are growing in either hospitable or inhospitable sites. Observation of this sort will help in the creation of good bonsai.

Figure 5 shows three white spruces I found on the seaward side of an island off the coast of Maine. Although the best seasons for collecting trees, as for transplanting any hardy plants, are early spring and fall, these were dug in mid-August, while we were on a family cruise. Not being prepared for plant collecting, we had only a penknife with which to pry them from the crevices in the granite and only the woodsy moss to protect their roots. When we got back to our boat, I removed about one-third of the branches to compensate in some measure for the roots lost in the uprooting, and I wrapped the moss-covered roots in plastic food bags. During the daytime we kept the plants in the cabin of the boat, sheltered from sun and wind. At night we put them on deck, where they were washed with dew and rain. After more than a week of this treatment, followed by a two-day trip home in the car, they were planted in sterilized potting soil and set under the bench in my greenhouse, a humid place away from direct sunlight. By October 15, they were in their permanent winter quarters in the plastic-paneled greenhouse shown in Figure 2. The fact that all three survived shows that if precautions are taken to avoid drying out,

Edmund B. Gilchrist, Jr.

FIG. 5. Naturally dwarfed white spruces, *Picea glauca,* collected on an island off the coast of Maine.

bonsai collecting is worthwhile under almost any conditions. Figure 5 was taken after the trees' first winter and shows them as collected and initially pruned.

Figure 6 shows the same three trees fifteen months later, planted in Japanese bonsai pots. The root systems are still more extended than they will finally be, which is why the pots are a little too big for the plants and the left-hand tree is in a somewhat awkward position. The dead branches enshrouded with the lichen called *Usnea* are typical of trees growing along the New England seashore, where they are constantly exposed to salt spray carried by winter gales. Preserving some branches is desirable to keep the bonsai in character; eliminating some is necessary to achieve simplicity. The choice of which to keep and which to cut away and the challenge of keeping the lichen alive in an unfriendly climate are the sort of things that make bonsai culture fascinating.

Natural bonsai in nurseries

Collecting natural bonsai need not be confined to rugged sites. Many promising specimens can be found in nurseries and greenhouses, bent and dwarfed by accident and neglect. Figure 7 shows

FIG. 6. The same trees as in Fig. 5 a year later. A little pruning and smaller containers have made them more decorative. (*opposite page*)

FIG. 7. I found this gnarled and twisted Hinoki cypress, *Chamaecyparis obtusa nana,* in a nursery specializing in dwarf plants.

a Hinoki cypress (*Chamaecyparis obtusa nana*) that I found in a small Connecticut nursery specializing in dwarf plants. The picture was taken soon after I brought it home and potted it, but before any attempt had been made to shape or prune it. The gnarled root and sparse foliage made the plant undesirable for a garden, but of unusual value to me. The nurseryman dug the plant with a very large ball of earth, most of which fell away quite easily. I had no trouble getting it into the six-inch azalea pot shown in the picture.

Artificially shaped bonsai

Historically, the next step after the collection of natural bonsai was the creation of artificially shaped plants. The techniques for artificial shaping are discussed in Chapter Two. They are so effective that there is almost no limit to the effects an expert can produce. The problem is where to stop. We are told that Japanese growers used to display their proficiency by creating grotesque forms with no counterparts in nature; and hideously distorted plants of this kind are sometimes offered as bonsai today. But the most satisfying bonsai are those that reflect natural forms.

The key to success is careful observation of trees and woody plants. An arboretum specimen will provide an ideal toward which the bonsai grower can work. A weather-beaten denizen of a mountain cliff or seashore rock will show how a tree uses its roots to cling to an inhospitable site and arranges its branches to achieve a precarious balance. An interest in bonsai will open up a new dimension of awareness to the plantsman as he drives through the country, cruises along the coast, or rides the chair lift at a ski resort.

Figure 8 shows a beautifully trained bonsai, *Zelkova serrata,* a species used extensively for dwarfing in Japan. This one is grown in the formal upright style, which closely mirrors the tree's natural growth. The tree is probably thirty or forty years old, with a height of about twelve inches and a trunk about two inches in diameter.

Edmund B. Gilchrist, Jr.

FIG. 8. This bonsai from the collection of R. Gwynne Stout is about 35 years old and was imported from Japan in 1958. It is *Zelkova serrata,* a deciduous tree which is a favorite of bonsai growers there.

It was grown as a bonsai from an early age and was imported about two years before the picture was taken. The tree is shown in July after the owner had thinned out a good deal of spring growth.

Results like this can be achieved only by study and practice. Buy enough cheap material so that you can experiment with a free hand, and do not hesitate to discard unsuccessful experiments. Also, do not hesitate to copy. Just as artists learn by copying masterpieces in museums, you will profit by trying to recreate the effects pictured in bonsai books. I keep on my workbench a Japanese booklet with pictures of fifty beautiful bonsai collected for the wedding of the Crown Prince. Before I begin to shape an unusual specimen, I page through this booklet to see what others have been able to do with similar arrangements of trunks and branches.

Also, success in shaping bonsai demands patience. Recent articles and books, perhaps in deference to the American insistence on prompt results, have stressed the idea that bonsai can be created in a single shaping session. With skilled practitioners this is sometimes the case; but with beginners, a year's work or sometimes several years' work is required to produce a truly decorative result.

At the first session I usually prune the tree quite severely, establish the approximate positions of its main branches, and plant it in a training pot. After a growing season, I often find that the new growth suggests a somewhat different pattern from that I originally had in mind. I prune and shape to this new pattern, wire the smaller branches into position, and move the tree to a bonsai container. As the years pass, the final form of the tree emerges. Sometimes, quite large branches must be moved or eliminated, the angle of the trunk changed, or a differently shaped pot provided. Creating a bonsai is not a single, definitive act; it is an evolutionary process. It took years for plants like those in the pictures to assume their present shapes. There are no short cuts to such results.

Plants for traditional bonsai

The following list of plants includes trees and shrubs I have found suitable for traditional bonsai. It is not by any means complete, but is intended merely for suggestion. Specialty nurseries often have a wide selection of dwarf and semidwarf varieties of many of these species, which often make interesting and authentic-looking bonsai. Dwarfs, however, do not always convey the same impression as their full size counterparts because their growth habit is quite different.

> *Acer buergerianum.* Trident maple
> *Acer campestre.* Hedge maple
> *Acer ginnala.* Amur maple
> *Abies* species. Fir
> *Betula alba.* White birch

Buxus species. Box
Calluna vulgaris. Heather
Carpinus caroliniana. American hornbeam
Carpinus japonica. Japanese hornbeam
Cedrus atlantica. Atlas cedar
Cedrus deodara. Deodar cedar
Chaenomeles japonica. Japanese quince
Chamaecyparis species
Cotoneaster species. Rock spray
Crataegus oxyacantha. English hawthorn
Crataegus phaenopyrum. Washington hawthorn
Cryptomeria japonica
Euonymus nana
Fagus grandifolia. American beech
Fagus sylvatica. English beech
Ginkgo biloba
Hedera helix. Ivy
Jasminum nudiflorum. Winter Jasmine
Juniperus species
Koelreuteria paniculata. Goldenrain tree
Liquidambar styraciflua. Sweet gum
Malus species. Crabapple
Photinia villosa
Picea species. Spruce
Pinus aristata. Bristlecone pine
Pinus cembra. Swiss stone pine
Pinus mugo mughus. Mugo pine
Pinus parviflora. Japanese white pine
Pinus strobus. White pine
Pinus thunbergi. Japanese black pine
Prunus species. Apricot, cherry, peach, plum
Pyracantha species. Firethorn
Quercus alba. White oak
Quercus coccinea. Scarlet oak

Quercus palustris. Pin oak
Quercus robur. English oak
Robinia pseudoacacia. Black locust
Rhododendron indicum. Indian azalea
Rhododendron mucronatum. Snow azalea
Rhododendron obtusum. Hirya azalea
Rhododendron Kurume hybrids
Salix blanda. Weeping willow
Styrax japonica. Japanese snowbell
Taxodium distichum. Bald cypress
Taxus species. Yew
Thuya occidentalis. American arborvitae
Thuya orientalis. Oriental arborvitae
Tsuga canadensis. Canadian hemlock
Ulmus americana. American elm
Ulmus parvifolia. Chinese elm
Ulmus pumila. Siberian elm
Wisteria floribunda. Japanese wisteria
Zelkova serrata

TROPICAL BONSAI FOR INDOOR GROWING

To some people, the word *bonsai* may seem a misnomer when applied to tropical plants, since the Japanese and Chinese did not use tropical material for this purpose. However, the orientals did use virtually all woody plants that would grow outdoors in their countries, including semitropical citrus and pomegranates; and I am sure they would have applied bonsai techniques to tropical trees and shrubs if they had had natural examples of tropical trees to emulate.

Moreover, I can find no word other than bonsai that carries with it the connotation of controlled size and shape, maturity, and decorativeness that this book emphasizes. So I will apply the word to all plants having these characteristics, regardless of their origin. The only broad category I will exclude will be herbaceous plants—those that do not have a woody stem—because by their nature they lack the permanence associated with bonsai.

Care of tropical bonsai

Interesting bonsai can be produced from almost all the small-leaved woody plants of the subtropics or tropics, and because of their rapid growth, you can obtain a decorative effect in a remarkably short time. The techniques are the same as for hardy plants, but they must be applied with proper regard to the difference in growth habits. For instance, hardy plants are dormant in winter, and training wires (see Chapter Two) can be left around their branches from early fall to spring without scarring the bark. In the case of tropical plants, growth continues throughout the year, except for a short time in the late fall and early winter, necessitating removal of wires after a few months. Also, the continuous and relatively rapid growth of tropical plants requires year-round pruning of the branches and, in some cases, of the roots as well; whereas hardy material needs pruning only in spring and summer and can sometimes go several years without repotting.

A collateral effect of their rapid growth is to make tropical bonsai less precious than hardy ones and, hence, less worrisome for beginners. It is not as distressing to lose through neglect a plant that can be duplicated in a year or two as to lose one that will take a decade to replace.

Enjoying tropical bonsai

For me the great attraction of tropical bonsai is that they will live indoors all year round, obviating the need for special winter arrangements and providing continuous interest for their owners. No matter what the temperature requirements of a tropical or semitropical plant, there will be some place in your house where it can pass the winter and be available for ceremonial visits to the mantel or coffee table. Subtropical trees, which need only to be protected from the frost, can live on an unheated sunporch or window sill. Natives of the true tropics will have to be closer to a radiator, perhaps in the kitchen or the bathroom. Knowledge of a plant's habitat plus careful observation of the night temperatures in different parts of your house will enable you to choose the right spot. If you develop an interest in any of the tropical plants pictured in this book, you will find cultural directions for growing plants indoors in *Garden in Your House*.

A good example of tropical bonsai is the *Serissa foetida variegata* shown in Figure 40. This Southeast Asian shrub is well suited to dwarfing by reason of its diminutive leaves and its equally diminutive flowers, one of which can be seen just to the left of the rock in the picture. The specimen in the picture has been grown indoors in a sunny window for two years. It requires frequent pruning, but will go for a surprisingly long time without repotting. The pot is one of three sold for serving hors d'oeuvres which I bought at Woolworth's. Directions for making a drainage hole in such a container will be found on page 110.

Tropical trees

Figure 9 shows *Calliandra surinamensis,* a tree grown extensively in the tropics. I bought this one by mail from a nursery in Florida. The shipping charges exceeded the cost of the tree, as it was planted in a gallon can in the wet, sandy soil which apparently prevails in that state. On arrival the tree was about four feet tall, unbranched, and quite leafless. I have had it for six years, and it is now just over two feet tall, planted in a six-inch Japanese pot and grown in a sunny window in winter. From April to September, I trim it with great regularity, trying not to let any of the shoots grow more than an inch. Once or twice each year I thin it out to show the pattern of the main stem and branches, a pattern you will see duplicated in pictures of trees on the plains of many tropical countries. At least once a year the tree is taken out of the pot and the root pruned as described in Chapter Three. It blooms frugally, off and on, throughout the summer and early fall.

FIG. 9. A tropical legume from South America, *Calliandra surinamensis,* grown six years as a bonsai.

FIG. 10. This tropical tree, *Jacaranda acutifolia,* is five years old. I grew it from seed, and keep it in the house during the winter and on the terrace in the summer.

Calliandra, like the jacaranda in Figure 10 and many other tropical trees, can be grown easily from seed and develops fast enough to make this procedure worthwhile. A two- or three-year-old tropical seedling makes an impressive bonsai, in contrast to most hardy seedlings, which can scarcely be trained for the first four or five years. If you want to grow hardy bonsai, you must for all practical purposes start with sizable plants. For tropical bonsai all you need is a seed catalogue and some idea of what kind of tree each seed will become.

Figure 10 is *Jacaranda acutifolia.* Like the calliandra, jacaranda is a leguminous plant from South America, easily grown from either seed or cutting, and suitable for house or greenhouse culture. The tree pictured is about five years old. Its roots have been spread over a flat rock and gradually and carefully exposed. This technique, described in more detail later in this chapter in "Group Plantings and Dish Gardens," seems particularly appropriate for tropicals, since many tropical trees grow naturally with exposed roots twining over rocks and ledges.

The large size of the leaves poses a real problem. On mature

Roche

FIG. 11. A tropical twining vine, *Oxera pulchella,* generally considered a greenhouse plant, but also satisfactory as a house plant on a sunny windowsill.

jacarandas the full leaf is more than twelve inches long, though the leaflets are quite minute. I have had some success in controlling leaf size by pinching out the tip of the leaf, but the most effective method is to induce budding by pinching the growing tips of branches and then removing the large, mature leaves as new, small ones appear.

The glazed container is dark blue, which makes a pleasant contrast to the lacy, light green foliage. It is twelve inches long, six inches wide, and an inch and a half deep, and has two large holes in the bottom for drainage.

A subtropical vine

In Figure 11 you will see an eight-year-old *Oxera pulchella,* a twining vine from New Caledonia. I acquired it as a small plant when I first began greenhouse gardening, with high hopes for its future as a flowering greenhouse vine. It has never flowered for me, and for the first few years of our coexistence I begrudged it the space it occupied and cut it back with ruthless abandon at the end of each flowerless summer. After four or five years of this treatment, it began to assume the graceful proportions and interesting root formation that now enable it to masquerade as a true oriental bonsai, trained in a semicascade style.

Gardenia grown as bonsai

Figure 1 shows one of my most decorative plants, a four-year-old gardenia. When I bought it, it was typical of those sold by florists and food stores at Easter, a graceless clump of branches interlaced with a spider web of green string and bamboo stakes and only temporarily redeemed by forced flowers. Pruning and training for two years have produced the results shown in the picture.

In the initial pruning, a number of main branches were removed. Most plants with opposite leaves and branches, like the gardenia, look better if this rigid symmetry is broken up.

The next step was to depress the main branches by wiring as described in Chapter Two. Like many tropicals, gardenias are difficult to shape in this manner. The wood is green and pliable and does not take a "set" as quickly as a hardy tree. After being held in the desired position for a whole season, a branch will often return nearly to where it was before training started. Several wirings are required for permanent bending. Also, because of the tenderness of the bark, it is necessary to wrap the wire with a protective covering. We have found the self-sealing, stretchable tape used by florists in making corsages to be satisfactory. It comes in green and brown, and most flower arrangers have a supply on hand. It should be used not only with gardenias, but when wiring other species with tender bark, such as jacaranda, citrus, pomegranate, and grevillea.

This gardenia grows in a southeasterly window sill on a metal tray filled with damp pebbles. A hot water radiator under the tray keeps the temperature high and fairly constant during the winter months. Gardenias do not grow well if they are subjected to very low temperatures or too many ups and downs. The year the picture was taken, the first flower opened on February 3, and blooming continued into early October.

The plant is in a rather deep pot with a dark blue glaze giving an impression of great weight, which is needed to balance the heavy foliage.

Miniatures

Miniatures, called Mame bonsai in Japan, are much more difficult to manage than larger plants. The minute root balls hold only a little water and present a relatively large area for evaporation, making drying out a constant danger. The only way I can manage really tiny plants like those in Fig. 13 (the right hand pot in that picture is one and a half inches high) is to grow them in a terrarium or under a glass dome covering a saucer filled with wet pebbles. I would advise beginners to start with sizable plants and save miniatures until they have had a year or two of experience.

The plant in Figure 12 is *Carissa grandiflora nana compacta,* commonly known as Natal plum. This one was a young plant scarcely more than a rooted cutting, which fortunately bloomed and set one luscious red fruit. While it probably would not be classed as a Mame bonsai by the Japanese, the mere placing of it in a Japanese pot with moss on the soil gave it somewhat the effect of a bonsai—neither gnarled nor venerable, to be sure—but undeniably decorative. Carissa is a tropical shrub from South Africa. In our southern states it is used for a hedge plant, as it withstands frequent shearing. Nurseries in Southern California and Florida sell large size plants which lend themselves to topiary shaping in the form of pyramids, cascades, or espaliers, or to training as full-sized bonsai.

The two plants in Fig. 13 are considerably more mature. The cotoneaster on the left is three years old. It originated as a cutting from one of my garden plants and has been grown in a cool greenhouse for the past two winters. From the very beginning, I pinched and pruned it frequently and kept it in a tiny pot with its roots well cut back so that it would be severely dwarfed.

The tiny leguminous tree on the right, *Leucaena glauca,* I grew from seed given me by a friend. Her specimen flowered and subsequently produced pea-like pods, one of which she sent me. The "peas" germinated within two weeks after I planted them. The picture was taken when the tree was about eighteen months old. From my experience to date, I believe this miniature will grow satisfactorily in the house, at least if kept under a bell jar most of the time.

A giant

In contrast to the miniatures, Figure 14 shows a seven-foot specimen of *Grevillea robusta,* a subtropical species widely grown as a street tree in parts of Southern California. Any plant this size requires comparatively little care. This particular one winters on my

Edmund B. Gilchrist, Jr.

FIG. 12. This Natal plum, *Carissa grandiflora nana compacta,* is less than one year old. The proportion of plant to container is very good.

sunporch and summers on my north terrace. The large root ball and glazed Japanese pot reduce evaporation to a minimum, so it will often go several days between waterings. Pruning at about six-week intervals is all that is needed to preserve its graceful shape. Of course, a tree like this in a large imported pot is expensive to buy, but for most indoor gardeners it will outlive a dozen smaller plants and provide more decoration to boot.

Grevillea is a good plant to remember no matter what size you have in mind. It is fast growing, but can be readily restrained by pinching and pruning. It tolerates cold down to the upper thirties, and an hour or two of daily sunlight in winter is all it really needs. I recommend it as a plant on which to practice bonsai techniques, with the hope that after a few years you would have something as attractive as this picture.

Roche

FIG. 13. Miniature bonsai, called Mame bonsai in Japan. Tiny plants in tiny pots are difficult to grow. These are *Cotoneaster dammeri* on the left and *Leucaena glauca* on the right.

FIG. 14. A semi-tropical tree, the silk oak, *Grevillea robusta,* twenty years old, seven feet high, grown for ten years as a large house plant bonsai.

Plants for tropical bonsai

The following is a list of woody plants native to the tropics and subtropics of the world which I have grown as bonsai indoors or in my greenhouse:

Acacia Baileyana
Bauhinia variegata
Calliandra surinamensis
Camellia japonica

Camellia sasanqua
Carissa grandiflora. Natal plum
Cassia eremophila. Shower tree
Citrus species. Orange, lemon, tangerine, lime, kumquat, calamondin
Cuphea hyssopifolia. Elfin herb
Cupressus arizonica. Arizona cypress
Cupressus macrocarpa. Monterey cypress
Delonix regia. Royal poinciana
Eugenia uniflora. Surinam cherry
Ficus diversifolia. Mistletoe fig
Ficus retusa. Indian laurel
Firmiana simplex. Chinese parasol tree
Gardenia jasminoides
Gardenia jasminoides radicans
Grevillea robusta. Silk oak
Hibiscus Rosa-sinensis Cooperi
Jacaranda acutifolia
Jasminum Parkeri. Jasmine
Leucaena glauca. White popinac
Malpighia coccigera. Miniature holly
Murraea exotica. Orange jasmine
Myrtus communis. Classic myrtle
Nicodemia diversifolia. Indoor oak
Ochna multiflora. Bird's eye bush
Olea europaea. Common olive
Oxera pulchella
Pistacia chinensis. Chinese pistachio
Pittosporum Tobira
Polyscias Balfouriana. Aralia
Polyscias fruticosa
Polyscias Guilfoylei
Punica Granatum nana. Dwarf pomegranate
Pyracantha species

Quercus suber. Cork oak
Schinus molle. California pepper tree
Serissa foetida
Trachelospermum jasminoides. Star jasmine

HERBACEOUS PLANTS DECORATIVELY GROWN

I excluded herbaceous plants from my definition of bonsai because they lack woody stems and are essentially short-lived. However, this does not mean that begonias, philodendrons, geraniums, African violets, and other herbaceous plants are not amenable to many of the same techniques of shaping and planting that are used in growing bonsai. In fact, plants of this kind offer as many opportunities for the application of good taste and horticultural skill as woody plants, and the results are equally decorative, as the photographs in this section will show.

Periodic replacement of herbaceous plants

The first point to be kept in mind is that herbaceous plants are, indeed, short-lived. In nature most are renewed annually either from seed or by new growth from the roots after the previous year's growth has died back in the dormant season. Outdoor gardeners recognize the need for periodic division of perennials, the purpose of which is to permit the development of new young roots. Indoor potted plants should likewise be renewed whenever they grow straggly. Learn to look at them as decorations and to discard or cut back those that are no longer pleasing to the eye. It is misplaced sentimentality to struggle with a scrawny philodendron because it was given to you by a dear friend or because it has stayed alive a surprisingly long time. It is false economy to nurse a drooping begonia in the hope that it may recover its former vitality. The first rule with herbaceous plants is: If it is not growing well, get rid of it.

In these soft-stemmed species, attractiveness depends in large measure on vigorous growth. Young, fast-growing foliage has a crispness and a vividness of color that are lacking in more mature, slower-growing leaves. I find that most of these plants grow more actively and produce more flowers in the first year, or at most the first three years, of their lives. All the plants pictured in this section are within that age bracket. When they begin to slow down and look tired, I reproduce them from seeds or cuttings and discard the parent plant, thus enjoying the same genetic stock for many generations. Those who are interested in this method of keeping a window garden perpetually young should read the sections on propagation in *Garden in Your House*.

Periodic replacement will not, of itself, insure vigorous growth. I pinch my plants back frequently, remove faded leaves and flowers daily, fertilize at least once a week in the growing season, and repot the plants whenever the containers are filled with roots. This keeps them growing fast and encourages the multiplication of side branches which, with good fortune, will bear flowers in season.

A gloxinia

Figure 15 shows a slipper gloxinia (*Sinningia speciosa*). It was

Edmund B. Gilchrist, Jr.

FIG. 15. A slipper gloxinia, *Sinningia speciosa,* grown in the house. The stake and wire are needed to support the overly long stems, which result from inadequate light.

grown on a south-facing window sill from seed planted eighteen months before the picture was taken, and in this time produced a tuber nearly three inches in diameter. After the first year of its life, it was dormant for about two months; so all the growth shown in the picture took place over a three-month period. As the two tall stems become ragged and stop flowering, they will be cut away to make room for those growing up from the bottom. After a total of six months or so, the plant will begin to lapse into dormancy once more. Then the stems and foliage should be cut away, the tuber gradually dried off, and the plant rested until the following season, when growth from the tuber will resume and the cycle can be repeated. Actually, when the plant becomes dormant, I will probably discard it for a smaller one reproduced from a leaf or seeds.

Professional gloxinia growers allow only one shoot to develop, thus producing a compact rosette of large oval leaves around a central crown of flowers. This technique works well in a greenhouse or under fluorescent lights, where the light intensity is fairly high and the light comes from overhead. For plants grown on a window sill without overhead light, I suggest letting a number of crowns develop as the picture shows.

Do not turn away from the picture without giving a moment's attention to the pot. It is an ordinary five-inch bulb pot, but I think you will agree that the proportions are much better than a standard flower pot and are particularly well suited to the foliage of this plant. Also, the pot is small enough to be unobtrusive. Too many otherwise handsome specimens are marred by a container of obtrusive size and ungainly shape.

Begonias

Figure 16 is *Begonia bartonea* 'Winter Jewel', a small fibrous begonia, photographed when it was about three years old, about twelve inches high, and looking its best. By accident, this plant illustrates the occasional virtue of really severe pruning. In the early spring of its second winter as a house plant, about ten months before the picture was taken, the plant fell and most of its foliage broke off, leaving only an inch or two of the old stems and a few new ones just starting. During the ensuing summer I put it in the shade of a dogwood tree, where it grew prodigiously. Two or three times during the summer the ends (two inches or so) were removed from the stems and major branches. This allows the light to reach the new growth near the base, encourages budding, and promotes the growth of new leaves. Since each leaf of a plant like a begonia lasts only six or eight months at the most, it is wise to start the winter with the youngest possible.

By September the plant had reached the balanced and graceful proportions shown in the picture, and it was time to find a suitable pot. I needed a relatively tall one to hold the lower leaves off the surface on which it stood and a delicate one to complement the fine lines of the foliage and flowers. My selection was a four-inch Italian terra-cotta pot. In over-all proportions it is not very different from a regular florist's pot; but its rolled lip, slightly convex

Edmund B. Gilchrist, Jr.

FIG. 16. A small fibrous rooted begonia, *B. bartonea,* 'Winter Jewel'. This fully mature plant is 12″ tall.

Edmund B. Gilchrist, Jr.

FIG. 17. This *Begonia venosa* is a much branched specimen, the result of frequent removal of tip growth. The pot is a Japanese bonsai dish 12" in diameter.

lines, and irregular texture make a world of difference in its appearance.

Admittedly, this plant is one-sided. So are all bonsai and most house plants. Except in shows, there is no advantage to perfectly symmetrical growth. I find the daily quarter revolution recommended by many texts to be time-consuming and often ineffective. In winter I turn my plants only as necessary to prevent complete topsidedness. I am satisfied to have a plant develop one attractive side, which can be turned to face the guests on state occasions.

Figure 17 shows a specimen *Begonia venosa,* a fibrous-rooted perennial from Brazil. Its large, pale green leaves are covered with fine white hairs; and its flowers, which it bears almost constantly, are pure white. Like many other hairy-leaved plants, it does well indoors because the hairs and the layer of still air which they

Edmund B. Gilchrist, Jr.

FIG. 18. This philodendron, *P. laciniatum,* has proven to be perennial. Year after year I cut away the old growth that ventures above the cork bark and am rewarded with new buds.

entrap insulate the leaves to a considerable extent from the dry air of the heated house. A similar insulation is provided in the so-called "glaucous" plants by the waxy layer that covers their leaves and gives them their characteristic whitish blue or grey color.

The plant in the picture is eighteen months old. At least a dozen plants have been propagated from it by tip cuttings, and this regular pruning accounts for its many branches. Unpruned specimens grow tall and thin and are reluctant to develop branches on their own. So, once more, I stress the benefits of pruning. When a tropical perennial is grown in the house and protected from drought and cold and devouring animals, there is nothing but the gardener's shears to remove the old growth and make space for the new.

The pot is an unglazed container about a foot in diameter. Its russet-brown color goes well with the color and texture of the leaves.

Philodendrons

I have seen more disreputable-looking philodendrons than any other kind of indoor plant. If ever there were plants that call for periodic drastic pruning or replacement, these are the ones. In nature, some species (like *P. laciniatum,* shown in Figure 18) are vines that clamber fifty or a hundred feet up the trunks of tropical trees in the rain forests of Central and South America. Others are tree-like "self-heading" kinds, with short internodes on their fleshy stems (like *P. McNeilianum,* shown in Figure 19).

This vigorous and ungainly habit of growth, while it makes philodendrons difficult for indoor gardeners to manage, is precisely what endears the genus to commerical growers. Their interest is in speed—the shortest time from cuttings to merchantable crop—uniformity, and economy of space. An example will show the lengths to which these considerations are pursued.

One winter a grower in the East trained his vining philodendrons on attractive grey driftwood instead of the usual slab of cedar bark. When he gave up the driftwood after a year's trial, I expressed

Edmund B. Gilchrist, Jr.

FIG. 19. A self-heading philodendron, *P. McNeilianum,* used as interior decoration in a Japanese jardiniere.

disappointment. His reason: instead of being able to fit the usual 120 finished plants into his delivery truck, he could only squeeze in 97 of those trained on driftwood. Furthermore, he could get a higher price for plants trained on cedar slabs, presumably because they were what the public expected.

The commercial grower sells his philodendron when the vines reach the top of the slab, i.e., when the plant is at its best. Any growth from this point on can only grasp in the air for something solid and, not finding it, flop over. The owner's normal response is to cut the vine off at the top of the slab, whereupon new growth appears just below the cut and the process is repeated. Meanwhile, the lower leaves mature and fall off, leaving a straggly tangle of stem and aerial roots.

One good solution is to abandon straggly plants that show more cedar bark than greenery. A satisfying alternative if you have the room is to cut the vines off an inch or two above the soil and wait for new growth from the bottom.

This latter technique was used on the plants pictured. The *P. laciniatum* is at least ten years old. Each year I prune it back to where I want new growth; and after the first of these drastic

FIG. 20. *Fuchsia* 'Victor Reiter', a hanging basket variety for spring and summer gardens.

prunings I replaced its cedar slab with a piece of cork bark, which is longer lasting and more attractive. The *P. McNeilianum* was cut off just above the roots a year before the picture was taken. The two buds below the cut then developed into growing points, making a more compact plant than the original. The whole process took the best part of a year, during which time the plant was in a four-inch clay pot under a bench in my greenhouse. Actually, it is still in that pot, which is considerably smaller than the handsome Japanese jardiniere shown in the picture. The pot is supported on an iron candle holder inside the jardiniere, so that water can drain freely from its roots.

The important point emphasized by these examples is that only artificial plants never lose their leaves. The life span of an individual leaf varies with the species. Some, such as philodendrons, rubber trees, and sansevieria, can be expected to hold a leaf three to four years. Others, like nasturtiums and geraniums, drop their leaves after only a few days or weeks. In nearly every case pruning the soft stems will produce the same effects as pruning the branches of woody species. New growth will appear from dormant buds below the cut, and, given good growing conditions, a bushier, more decorative plant will develop. (See Chapter Two.)

Hanging baskets

All my hanging baskets are planted the same way, whether they are for winter use in the house, summer use on the terrace, or year-round use in the greenhouse. My method is to line the basket with sheet moss and then fill it with damp sphagnum. (The sheet moss is not necessary, but makes the basket look neater in the early stages before the branches begin to trail down and hide the container.) Having packed in the sphagnum tightly, I literally stuff the plants into it, taking care that the sphagnum is firm around the root ball. If it is not, the roots will not absorb moisture from the moss or grow out into it, since the roots of most plants will not extend themselves across a cavity.

The fuchsia basket pictured in Figure 20 was planted with three rooted cuttings in April, four months before the picture was taken. From the time it was planted, it hung outside in filtered sunlight. In such a situation, there is great risk that the basket will dry out, and I make it a rule to see that the exterior moss never feels dry, even if this means three waterings on hot, windy days. Plantings of this kind can scarcely be overwatered, since any excess drains away quickly. I dissolve fertilizer in the water about once a week.

Fuchsias do not bloom much in the winter. They need the long days of spring and summer to set flower buds. For this reason, when the fall nights begin to grow long and cold, I let my fuchsias dry out in their baskets or pots in a frost-free location until they lose their leaves and go completely dormant. Thereafter, I water them once every two or three weeks.

In January or February I move them into the greenhouse, where they soon revive. Then, as soon as there is enough new growth,

I take cuttings for my baskets, since I have found that with fuchsias new plants are best for this kind of planting. With some other genera, notably begonias and ferns, you can plant baskets with mature, droopy plants, obtaining a full, pendulous effect almost at once.

Watering hanging baskets is more of a problem indoors than out because of the dripping. However, this last only a few minutes —not hours as some apprehensive gardeners seem to fear. I try to hang my baskets over a plant tray where dripping will do no harm. If this is not practical, I put a bucket or tray under the plant until the drops stop falling. An even safer method is to water the baskets on the kitchen drainboard or in the bathtub. In any event, a ten minute soaking in a sink or tub once or twice a week is desirable for baskets growing both inside and out, to insure their being wet through.

Plants for hanging baskets

There are many plants that lend themselves to growing in hanging baskets. My favorites are:

> *Abutilon megapotamicum*
> *Aeschynanthus*—several species
> *Asparagus Sprengeri.* Asparagus fern
> *Begonia*—practically all species and varieties
> *Browallia speciosa*
> *Chlorophytum* species. Spider plant
> *Columnea*—any trailing species
> *Davallia* species
> *Episcia*
> *Hypocyrta*
> *Lantana montevidenis.* Trailing lantana
> *Lobelia erinus*

Edmund B. Gilchrist, Jr.

FIG. 21.   Geraniums, *Pelargonium hortorum:* Two years old, six years old, and three months old.

Nephrolepis. Boston ferns, particularly the fluffy types
Pelargonium peltatum. Ivy geranium
Polypodium aureum
Saintpaulia, trailing hybrids. Trailing African violet
Schizocentron elegans. Spanish shawl
Sedum Morganianum. Burro tail
Tropaeolum majus. Nasturtium
Verbena peruviana. Verbena Peruvian flame
Viola tricolor. Pansy

Geraniums

Figure 21 shows how geraniums look at different ages and when differently grown. On the right is a group of three plants in their first summer, made from cuttings rooted in January and grown by a specialist in a greenhouse. They are bushy, vigorous, and replete with flower buds—the kind of plants sold by the million each spring and summer. On the left is a single plant a year older than those on the right. It grew vigorously its first summer, was cut back severely during the winter, rested, and now, in its second summer, is big enough to fill the pot by itself. The middle plant is at least six years old and has never been pinched or pruned. It may have sentimental value to its owner, but it can hardly be called satisfying horticulturally or aesthetically. If you want blossoms this high in the air, you can get more of them in a year's time by growing a standard geranium as described in "Potted Topiary, Standards and Cascades," below.

The first lesson to be learned from these plants is that the surest way to have vigorous, decorative geraniums on your terrace or in your garden in the summer is to buy or propagate new plants each year. (This is one instance where the commercial grower can produce a better result than the average amateur.)

The second lesson is that if you want to keep your plants for subsequent summers, you must cut them back and rest them for two or three months during the winter. This means keeping the pots in a cool (40° F. to 60° F.), well-lighted place and watering them every two weeks or so. With this treatment they become semi-dormant and are usually easy to revive.

Our grandmothers used to hang their geraniums bare-rooted and upside down in their cellars for the winter. The cellar was cool and damp, not heated like ours, so the plants usually did not dry out. They did, however, become completely dormant and were sometimes impossible to revive.

In very early spring the plants should be repotted. Do this when the soil is quite dry. Squeeze all the old soil away from the roots, replace it with a fresh, sterilized mixture, and put the plants in a sunny place. By May they should be ready for the garden.

The final lesson from the picture is not to move the geraniums from your summer garden directly to your winter window sill. By summer's end they are too tall to be decorative. If you want geraniums in the winter, cut back your summer plants or take cuttings from them in July. Grow them in full sun during the rest of the summer, and they should become attractive by December.

African Violet Magazine

FIG. 22. A blue ribbon winning African violet, *Saintpaulia* 'Beaming', grown by Mrs. C. B. Ward.

The white container on the right is a chimney liner usually carried in stock by the building material suppliers who sell sand, gravel, drainage tiles, and the like. It is cheap and decorative, but it has no bottom whatsoever and is practical only for use outdoors in a place where it will not have to be moved during a summer's growing season.

African violets

I suppose that more African violets are grown by indoor gardeners than any other plant. There are African violet societies throughout the country, and a quarterly magazine devoted to their culture is published by the African Violet Society of America. The prize specimens exhibited at the Society's national shows are magnificently decorative, well illustrated by Figure 22, a picture of the 1960 Silver Cup winner. However, in spite of all this interest and information, we see a surprising number of homely specimens in houses and offices. Since this is usually the result of letting the plants take care of themselves, a few words about the proper way to grow them may not be out of place.

The amount of light available to the plants is important. While violets are properly called shade plants, remember that the fall and winter sun has no more intensity indoors than high summer shade. These plants do best for me in windows that have two or three hours of sun from November through January and in sunless windows with an unobstructed view of the sky during the other months. If you want to keep them in a sunny window all year round, you will find that a very thin curtain or an ordinary screen provides enough shade in spring and summer. Violets will also develop to perfection under fluorescent lights, the ideal arrangement being two four-foot, 40-watt tubes set eight inches above the foliage of the plants to produce about 450 foot-candles.

As for other elements in the environment, the relative humidity should be at least 30 per cent; the temperature should be steady and somewhere between 65° F. and 75° F. in the daytime with a 5° to 10° drop at night, in any event not below 60° F.; and the growing medium should be firm enough to support the plant and spongy enough to hold moisture and allow air to reach the root ends.

Pruning techniques for African violets differ from those followed with the other species discussed in this book. The desired result, as the picture shows, is a circular shape with the leaves radiating from a central rosette like the spokes of a wheel. This is achieved, not by pinching the tip, but by removing all other points of growth from the main stem as they appear. You can do this by scratching them out with a knife or with your fingernail. The trick is to remove them when they are very small. If they are allowed to reach an appreciable size, there will be gaps in the circle of leaves when they are removed.

Violets have stems like any other plant. As they grow old, these stems get straggly and then floppy. At this stage the plant is no longer decorative. The thing to do is cut off the top whorl of leaves with an inch or so of stem and put it in your propagating box, where it will root in a month or six weeks. Throw the rest of the plant away.

A well-grown African violet should be set off by a handsome pot. My own partiality is for clay. Its texture and color are generally more harmonious to the foliage and flowers than plastic. I find that my plants grow best if the clay is unglazed and look best if the pot is wider than it is high. The so-called "chubby" florist's pots or round bonsai pots are about right.

One other comment. It is not necessary to wrap the pot or its rim in aluminum foil to prevent petiole rot. If you are bothered by this fungus disease, dip the rim of your clay pots in melted paraffin for a few seconds before you plant the violet. Even without this precaution, weekly washing of the pot rim will generally control the disease.

A terrestrial fern

The growth habit of *Lygodium scandens,* pictured in Fig. 23, is typical of a large group of ferns, including maidenhairs, Boston

Roche

FIG. 23. Interesting driftwood, a blue Japanese pot and a climbing fern, *Lygodium scandens*.

ferns, the genus *Pteris,* and some species of the genus *Pellaea.* They are characterized by long-lived perennial root systems, either wiry or fibrous, and fronds which last one year, or more correctly, one growing season. They do not quite fit into either the woody or the herbaceous plant group, and they are also somewhat different from the epiphytic ferns described later on.

The important rule with these plants is to cut away the fronds when they first begin to dry up and turn brown. I remove all the old fronds in the summer as soon as I see tiny fiddleheads pushing up from the roots. This leaves nothing to detract from the delicate purity of the new fronds as they unfold. The fern in the picture is a good example of the results. It was completely cut back in early August, and the picture was taken the second week in October.

The driftwood through which the fronds are entwined is a piece of cedar. It is secured in the blue Japanese bonsai pot by wire running through the two drainage holes and through a hole in the wood.

The fern itself needs a surprisingly small amount of soil. Every two or three years I remove it from the container, divide the plant (if it is potbound), just as you would divide a garden perennial, and replant a division in the same container. In the alternate years, I simply cut away all the old fronds as described above.

This decorative plant will grow quite satisfactorily indoors if the temperature and humidity are reasonably high. Because of its twining fronds, it must have some sort of trellis for support.

SUCCULENTS IN ORNAMENTAL CONTAINERS

Cacti are uniquely suited to indoor decoration. Their shapes and colors go well with modern houses. They grow slowly and retain their proportions for years. They will tolerate equally the dry heat of a south picture window and the cold, dim light of an unheated north window, provided the temperature does not go below 40° F. They do not need the daily watering that other plants demand. Indeed, since they pass the winter in a dormant or semidormant state, particularly when the light is poor, they need little or no water; and the real problem is to avoid giving them too much.

One thing must be kept in mind. Even a cactus cannot stay dormant forever. If you keep yours in a dark corner in the winter, you must give it at least three months of direct sun in the summer, so that root and top growth can take place. And you must accustom the plant gradually to the sun, either by moving it to successively brighter spots or by shading it at first during the mid-day hours. If you do not observe this precaution, an incurable case of sunburn may result. The stems will develop permanently disfiguring brown splotches or streaks.

Some agaves and euphorbias and other desert plants with woody stems and stiff leaves go into winter dormancy just as cacti do.

Edmund B. Gilchrist, Jr.

FIG. 24. This four foot organ-pipe cactus, *Lemaire-ocereus,* is dusty blue. It requires little care and grows only about three inches a year.

Edmund B. Gilchrist, Jr.

FIG. 25. Succulent plants, *Echeveria derenbergi*, in a white pottery bowl.

They need about the same treatment as cacti. But the fleshy, soft-leaved succulents insist upon growing instead of sleeping and must be given as much winter sun as possible. Without good light they grow leggy and leafless. In fact, their requirements are about the same as those of other herbaceous plants.

A large cactus

The remarkable cactus in Figure 24 is a *Lemaireocereus* species about four feet tall. It is growing in an ordinary bulb pan painted a blend of powder blue and grey to match the color of the plant. Keeping a cactus of this size upright when it is first put in a shallow pot is a formidable problem. Cacti get along on surprisingly few roots, and even these few shrivel up when the plant becomes dormant, so the root ball is neither large nor solid. When we planted the cactus in the picture, we tied it in place with copper wire passed through extra holes we had drilled in the bottom of the pot and over the base of the roots. Some of this wire can be seen crossing the exposed roots in the picture. If the roots had seemed tender, we would have put leather pads between them and the wire.

This plant shows how much more decorative a cactus is when it branches. Not all species branch freely, but most can be induced to do so if they are pruned when they are young. Pruning a cactus consists of cutting it off at the place you want branches. From one to four new growing points will develop below the cut.

Small succulents

Figure 25 is *Echeveria derenbergi* (painted lady), with pale green, almost white, leaves, each of which has a pink tip. The flowers are orange and appear off and on throughout the spring and summer. It is typical of many species and varieties of succulents of the crassula family native to the American deserts. The plant is two years old and was moved into this white pottery bowl with a large drainage hole six months before the picture was taken. At that time, several of the longest stems were pruned, and new ones have grown out to replace these. The soil surface is covered with small white stones. This planting remained attractive for about a year and then grew leggy and unattractive. I rerooted each tip and in a month or two had the makings of a new arrangement to serve as a decorative accessory for another indoor year.

Incidentally, this picture illustrates the virtue of confining succulent plantings to a single species, either one large plant or a number of smaller ones. It is tempting to mix a variety of succulents in one arrangement, but the results are seldom satisfying for more than a few months. If the plants would stand still, all would be well; but different growth rates quickly spoil the proportions unless great care is taken in selecting species that grow alike.

EPIPHYTES ON DRIFTWOOD

In the rain forests of the tropics, where plant life is engaged in a struggle for light, plants that have neither trunks to thrust upward nor vining stems to climb the trunks of others have taken to growing high up in trees and on rocky ledges. Unlike parasites, which penetrate the wood of their host plant and rob it of moisture and nutrients, these epiphytes use their host merely as a resting place. Their roots function primarily, if not exclusively, as anchors and are therefore called "holdfast" roots. Apparently, it is the leaves and stems that take up moisture and nutrients.

FIG. 26. An epiphytic fern, *Davallia Griffithiana*, growing on a piece of grey weathered cedar.

Epiphytes can be induced to grow in the house or greenhouse on cork bark or driftwood, producing an effect that is at once decorative and suggestive of their natural habitat. There are two requisites for a successful planting. First, the plant must be firmly anchored, so that the holdfast roots can find their way into crevices without being pulled loose. Second, the holdfast roots must be given a damp surface to grow on and must themselves be kept damp while they are growing. I fulfill these requirements in the case of epiphytic ferns by packing the roots into a well-drained cavity in a piece of driftwood, often one I have hollowed out myself. The best packing material is osmunda fiber, the wiry black roots of osmunda ferns. The same technique will work with bromeliads, or you can anchor them to the unbroken surface of driftwood or bark by covering the roots with a pad of osmunda and wiring it firmly in place. Some growers use a strip of nylon stocking or plastic tape instead of wire. They work just as well, but they tend to look messy.

Whatever your system of anchoring, keep the osmunda damp around the roots for three or four months until new ones grow and attach themselves. After this, bromeliads need watering less often. The wetter the roots are kept, the better the plants will grow; but I find that several days' neglect will not do them any serious harm, provided their "cups" are full of water. Epiphytic ferns can also be left for two or three days without water in an emergency.

It is interesting that of all the tropical epiphytes and semi-epiphytes raised in pots, only orchids have traditionally been grown in a medium such as osmunda, which duplicates the spongy, fibrous material in which they grow naturally. Bromeliads, epiphytic ferns, many gesneriads, some begonias, philodendrons, anthuriums, and countless other tropical plants will thrive in osmunda or sphagnum moss, both of which can be mounded above the rim of a container and watered freely without washing away. All that is necessary in growing plants in such a medium is regular feeding during the growing season with a weak solution of a quick-acting, water-soluble fertilizer.

Epiphytic ferns

The piece of wood in Figure 26 was part of a stump found on a lake shore in the Adirondacks. As cut, it stands fifteen inches high and is about six inches in diameter at the base. We prepared the wood for planting by hollowing out a cavity two inches in diameter in the center of the piece, drilling a one-inch drainage hole through the bottom, and giving it a coat of colorless wood preservative inside and out. Be sure to use a preservative with a zinc naphthanate base; pentachlorophenol, the other popular active agent, is lethal to plants for months. (Copper naphthanate is also safe for plants, but leaves a dark green stain on the treated wood.)

The fern in the picture is *Davallia Griffithiana*. The happiest thing about any planting of this particular species on weathered cedar is the harmony between the silver-grey of the wood and the greyish-white of the fern's rhizomes. If the wood is treated with preservative, it will hold its color for years.

Almost the only care required by the fern, aside from regular watering and fertilizing, is the removal of dead fronds. In all davallias the individual fronds last about a year. This species drops its fronds and renews them one by one over a period of several months. Other davallias drop all their fronds at nearly the same time and develop a whole new crop several weeks later.

Epiphytic ferns that I have grown successfully on driftwood are: *Aglomorphia coronans, Asplenium nidus, Davallia* species, *Platycerium* species, *Polypodium aureum, Stenochleana palustris.*

Bromeliads

Figure 27 shows the kind of effect that can be obtained by planting bromeliads on interesting pieces of wood. It happens that these three pieces are quite small, and there is only one plant on each. However, you can use a number of plants of the same or different species on larger pieces, and I have planted trees six or seven feet high with as many as fifteen different kinds of bromeliad. Bromeliad plantings are quite long-lived, so it is worthwhile to spend time and money getting an attractive piece of wood and planting it carefully. Remember, however, that it is the plant that lasts from year to year and not the individual rosettes. These will generally last only a year or two and will then bear a flower and die. They should be cut away as soon as they begin to wither, leaving space for the new offsets that will develop in their places.

The planting on the left is *Billbergia Lietzei,* a semidwarf. In this species the typical bromeliad offsets travel an inch or two away from the original plant before developing into a new rosette. You can see one at the lower right of the picture pointing upwards and to the right. This habit of growth makes *B. Lietzei* appropriate where there is a considerable length of wood for it to grow along. *Aechmea* 'Foster's Favorite' and many others have the same way of growing.

Edmund B. Gilchrist, Jr.

FIG. 27. Bromeliads on driftwood are decorative and easy to keep in the house. Left to right: *Billbergia Lietzei*, *B. Saundersi*, and *Tillandsia ionantha*.

The piece of wood was found along a stream in the Pocono Mountains of Pennsylvania and is particularly well suited for planting because it will sit comfortably on a table or mantelpiece. In the winter I keep it on a window sill when it is not on display, and in summer I keep it on the ground under some lacy shrubbery.

The bromeliad at the upper right is another billbergia, *B. Saundersi*. As the picture shows, this species is somewhat larger than *B. Lietzei*. It forms a tighter clump and is more apt to stay where it is planted. Its leaves are more colorful, a smoky purple with lighter transverse bands.

We made this planting five years before the picture was taken. It hangs in a south window in winter and against the outside of the east wall of the house in summer. The better the light, the more vivid the color of the leaves. Its over-all height is about fifteen inches; it hangs by a wire, which is hidden behind the large central leaf in the picture.

The miniature at the lower right is *Tillandsia ionantha*. Its minute rosettes are a bluish-grey color, particularly if it is grown in good light. In the spring the tips turn quite red, and a blue flower appears from the center of the rosette. When the flower has faded, a number of new rosettes form around the original one, enlarging and tightening the clump.

Edmund B. Gilchrist, Jr.

FIG. 28. Twenty-nine Amur maple seedlings, *Acer ginnala*, planted with rocks and moss in a homemade concrete container.

The specimen in the picture is planted on a piece of cedar dug from a peat bog in New Jersey. It has spent the last four winters hanging with the *B. Saundersi* in my south-facing window garden, right against the pane. I water it every day by dipping the entire planting in the watering can.

T. ionantha, which has no common name, grows slowly and takes longer than most bromeliads to anchor itself firmly. I hold them in place by passing a length of copper or galvanized wire over the juncture between two rosettes and through holes in the wood. Then instead of tightening the wire (which might cut the plant in two), I poke osmunda under the plant to hold moisture and encourage the development of roots. The best tool for this purpose is a chopstick, procurable at stores that carry oriental goods. I find a supply of pointed, wooden chopsticks indispensable.

GROUP PLANTINGS AND DISH GARDENS

At the mention of dish gardens, most of my American readers will think of the florist's mixture of tropical foliage plants grouped in a fancy container. A Japanese might envisage a miniature landscape in perfect scale down to the tiniest detail. An English gardener might think of dwarf, hardy trees and shrubs planted in a soapstone sink.

Whichever your preference, you should bear in mind that there are only a few plants which can live any length of time in drainless containers and poor light. If you want to leave your dish garden continuously on display in such conditions, you should consider it no more than a long-lasting flower arrangement. Choose expendable plants, and discard them when they begin to look poorly.

On the other hand, if you want to keep your group planting from year to year, use a container with drainage holes and keep the planting in good light during the day.

All the groups pictured in this section have one thing in common: each is composed of but a single species. This, of course, is not a necessity. However, as in the case of the succulents already discussed, confining a planting to one species avoids the problem of different growth rates and cultural requirements. Also, I find the restrained effect particularly satisfying.

Group plantings, like single-specimen bonsai and herbaceous plants, vary in length of life. The maples, calliandras, Chinaberries, and junipers in Figures 28, 29, 30 and 31 are more or less permanent. All of them can be trained over the years into decorative shapes and could be classed as bonsai. The dish gardens in Figure 32 will last a year or two with surprisingly little change, but will finally need replanting.

Seedlings for group plantings

To create immediate bonsai, you will often find it cheaper and more satisfactory to plant groups of seedlings rather than mature plants. Maples and spruces are perhaps the most commonly used, but any kind of tree that grows naturally in forests or groves would be appropriate. The planting in Figure 28 is composed of Amur maples (*Acer ginnala*). The seedlings were about a year old when they were planted, which was three months before the picture was taken.

Roche

FIG. 29. Tiny tropical trees, *Calliandra surinamensis,* in a flat bonsai dish with their roots trained over a rock.

It is fairly easy to propagate most maples by sowing the seed outdoors or in your cold frame in a carefully prepared bed in the fall. If it is not disturbed or allowed to become dry, you should have strong seedlings the following spring.

As an alternative, you can buy the seedlings from any of the numerous nurseries that specialize in supplying them. If you order in lots of fifty or a hundred, you will find them surprisingly cheap, and you will have plenty to work with and some spares in case not all of them live. They will be delivered in winter or early spring, bare-rooted, leafless, and wrapped in damp sphagnum moss. They should be potted or planted within two days after arrival. For the initial training containers, I use 2 ¼ -inch clay pots.

Whichever way you get your seedlings, remember to prune the roots and tops drastically when you first put them into training containers. I generally cut off the trunk four or five inches above the ground and cut away any long trailing roots. In this process, I often find that the seedling's trunk gets thicker for about two inches below the original ground line, and there is sometimes an attractive curve in that two-inch stretch. In such cases, I plant the seedling with the thickest part of its trunk just at ground level, removing any roots above this point. If there happens to be a large root near the point of maximum diameter, I put that at ground level and start to train it along the surface.

After the seedlings have been in their pots a month or so, most will begin to leaf out, and all those that are going to survive will have formed new compact roots and will be ready for planting.

Arranging the plants in the group

You will find the arrangement of a group of plants in a container more difficult than you would expect. Patience is essential; an artistic eye is an advantage; and knowledge of the rules developed by Japanese bonsai growers will prove helpful. These rules are set forth at length with excellent diagrams in the book *Miniature Trees and Landscapes* by Yoshimura and Halford. The most important are: use an odd number of trees

in each cluster; arrange the three principal trees in an uneven tri-
angle; fit the others between them; and remember that the trees
on the outside of the group or along the edges of clearings will
naturally slant outward in search of light, while those in the center
will naturally reach up higher for the same reason.

Homemade containers

The maples in Figure 28 are in a homemade concrete container.
To produce these, we make wooden forms for the outside and
inside of the container walls. The outside form is as high as we
want the container; the inside form is lower than the outside by
the thickness of the container bottom, say, seven-eighths of an inch.
The distance between the forms when one is placed inside the other,
i.e. the thickness of the container walls, is also about seven-eighths
of an inch. The outside form is held together by screws and the
inside by battens so as to permit easy removal after the concrete has
hardened. The corners of the inside forms are rounded.

The material we use is ready-bagged concrete mix sold for patch-
ing walks. Before you wet the mix, put the outside form on a flat
board or a piece of plywood and tack it in place with nails. Nail
large corks to the bottom board where you want drainage holes.
Then mix the concrete and pour it inside the form and around the
corks to make the bottom of the container. (We generally use wires
or metal lath as a reinforcement, but this is probably not necessary.)

When the bottom has reached the desired thickness, insert the
inside form which will rest on the bottom. Then pour the sides
of the container.

After the concrete has set for twelve or eighteen hours, gingerly
remove the forms. The concrete should still be soft enough so you
can obliterate blemishes and round the corners with a trowel or
putty knife. Also, you can run a wire brush over the outside to
produce an attractive rough surface. If you find any imperfections,
mix a little more concrete and plaster them up before the main
structure sets.

Let the container cure another six to twelve hours before lifting it off the bottom board or attempting to remove the corks, and during this period spray the concrete lightly with water three or four times to prevent cracking. When the container has cured a total of at least twenty-four hours, soak it in a dark pink solution of potassium permanganate—the druggist can get it for you—for two or three days to neutralize its acidity. Then let it dry for a week, after which it will be ready for planting.

Choice and care of plants

The reason I chose Amur maples for the planting in the picture is that they have fairly small leaves which are not as likely to become spotted or blemished as some of the other small-leaved maples. Also, the Amurs have striking red-winged fruits and spectacular coloring in the fall. They are very hardy and must be kept quite cold in winter. They might withstand one or two warm winters when their growth was not interrupted by dormancy, but continuous treatment of this kind would probably kill them.

My planting spends the winter in an unheated cold frame, where it is protected from drying winds. If such a space were not available, I would bury the entire planting in the ground with only the top three or four inches of the trees protruding and would cover it with a mulch of pine needles or other similar material.

Tropical trees on a rock

The calliandras in Figure 29 are cuttings from the plant in Figure 9. We planted them on the rock about two years before the picture was taken, after they had spent two or three months in small pots. Now that they are well established, they should grow satisfactorily on a window sill or in a greenhouse at temperatures between 50° F. and 70° F. The long, flat dish is an unglazed dark brown bonsai tray from Japan. It has five drainage holes and cost twenty-five dollars.

Technique of planting on rocks

This is just one example of the many different effects obtainable with rock plantings. You can use low, flat rocks like the one in the picture and surround them with moss or ferns to suggest a rocky outcrop in a savanna or with white sand to suggest a rocky island. Or you can use an upright rock to suggest a mountain or cliff. The roots of the plant can be confined in natural crevices, so that the rock acts as a container, or they can be trained and exposed over the rock and into the surrounding soil. You can use either hardy material reminiscent of the mountains or the seaside cliffs in our summer resorts or tropical material to give the effect of a jungle scene.

There is almost no tree or shrub that cannot be induced to grow on a rock if you are patient, and any rock that catches your fancy will probably be satisfactory. In general, however, I would keep my eye trained for dark-hued, hard-looking rocks with crannies to hold pockets of soil and moss. A flat bottom is essential. Seashore rocks, which are often excellent for the purpose, must be soaked in fresh water for several months before use.

If the rock has a natural crevice to hold the roots, you can follow the normal rules for planting outlined in Chapter Three. If you are going to train the roots over the rock and then expose them as in Figures 10 and 29, use the special techniques described in the following paragraphs.

To prepare the rock for planting, fasten three or four twists of copper wire on it to hold the tree and its main roots in place. Each twist consists of a piece of copper wire two or three inches long, bent double, with the bend glued to the rock. As a fastener we use epoxy cement, available in various mixtures and forms. Inquiry at the hardware store may turn up other adhesives equally suitable.

When you have a suitable rock with wires in position, the next step is to select the plant material and decide how it should be placed. If you are going to plant a group, keep in mind the basic rules outlined above in the discussion of the Amur maples. If it is to be a single tree, the rules set forth in Chapter Three for locating the plant in relation to the container will apply. But in either case you will probably have to make some adjustment to get the roots to fit comfortably over the rock.

Rock planting requires complete baring of the roots and should therefore be done in the fall or early winter when the plant is dormant. Remove as much of the soil as you can with gentle crumbling motions of the fingers; then, soak the roots in water and wash the remaining soil away. If the tree has been raised in a pot, you may find the roots intertwined and growing in circles. They should be carefully untangled and straightened out.

Now settle the tree on the rock, working the junction of the roots down as close to the rock surface as possible and spreading the main roots out, so that they radiate from the bole. A minimum of three such radiating roots is essential for a secure planting. During this operation be sure that the roots never become dry. It is a good idea to keep some wet paper or sphagnum moss at hand to cover them with when you pause in your work.

When you have decided where each root is to lie on the rock, smear these places with a glue made of clay (usually to be found in the subsoil of the garden), peat moss, and water. Set the roots in this glue; pack more of it on top of the roots; and where the roots run through a wire twist, protect them with small wads of osmunda fiber or bits of leather. Tightening the twists over the roots should then produce a steady planting. If the plant is still wobbly, try wrapping more wire completely around the roots and the stone —again with osmunda or leather pads to protect the living tissues. Do not slight this part of the job. An absolutely firm anchorage is the key to success.

When the plant has been anchored, lead the roots into the soil if the planting is to be in a bonsai dish, or cut them short if the rock is to be the container. In either case, paint the roots with the peat-clay glue along their entire exposed length and cover them with a layer of green woods moss, which will adhere firmly to the glue. This will keep the peat and clay from washing away, will protect the roots from drying out, and will add to the beauty of the planting. No matter how great the temptation, do not begin to remove the moss and expose the roots for six to eight months. Then do it gradually, and preferably when the plant is dormant. Start by uncovering the roots where they join the trunk, and work outwards in stages a month or two apart, cutting away the smaller roots and leaving a few large ones. Be careful at each stage not to expose or remove a great many of the new, white roots at the ends of the root branches. These are the so-called "feeding roots" through which water is absorbed and from which new growth develops. If too many are cut away or permitted to dry out, the plant will die.

Another group of tropical trees

The planting in Figure 30 is *Melia Azedarach,* the Chinaberry. This group is composed of eight six-month-old seedlings. To start it I bought a fifty-cent packet of seeds, which yielded thirty or forty seedlings in a short time. The little plants grew with great vigor in my 55° F. greenhouse. From the start I kept them small by frequent pinching and by confining the roots in two-inch pots.

Roche

FIG. 30. Eight Chinaberry tree seedlings, *Melia Azedarach,* only six months old.

The trees are planted in a very shallow Japanese dish with the usual drainage holes. Because the dish had less depth than a two-inch pot, it was necessary to soak the root balls in water and remove the soil as though for a rock planting in order to spread the roots out flat. The placing of the trees follows the rules discussed in connection with the Amur maples. There are two clusters, one of five and the other of three, arranged to suggest a natural rocky grove.

The Chinaberry has naturalized itself in many tropical and subtropical countries, probably as a result of the extreme viability of the seeds and the vigor of the seedlings. Because it is tropical, it must be kept in a house or greenhouse during the winter months in the northern half of the country. When the plants in the picture are more mature, they will be slower growing and will not need pruning so often; and I would hope that they would flower and bear the berries that gave them their name.

Repotting group plantings

When the times comes for repotting a planting like the maples and the Chinaberries, the rocks can be lifted out and the entire group treated as a single plant. By that time all the roots will have grown into a tight mass and should hang together when out of the pot. (For techniques see Chapter Three.)

A Japanese landscape

The miniature landscape shown in Figure 31 was created by a person with great talent and experience. The plant material and accessories are all obtainable in this country. The dish is a hand-made American ceramic piece, with drainage holes of course. The tiny figures and the bridge, while made in Japan, were bought in a Japanese-American gift shop. The trees are little more than rooted cuttings of juniper, and the ground is carpeted with moss from the woods. The stream is white sand, the kind sold for pet birds.

This planting is a lesson in restraint. There are just enough accessories to suggest the scale, not so many as to distract attention from the over-all effect of the rock and the trees.

A planting like this may be kept any place where it can be best enjoyed; for if any of the plant material dies, it can easily be replaced.

Edmund B. Gilchrist, Jr.

FIG. 31.   A dish garden in perfect scale. From the collection of R. Gwynne Stout.

Edmund B. Gilchrist, Jr.

FIG. 32. The only plants in this book in drainless containers. Care must be taken to avoid overwatering. *Scindapsus aureus, Sansevieria trifasciata Laurenti, Peperomia hederifolia.*

Dish gardens

Figure 32 shows three dish gardens in drainless containers: pothos (*Scindapsus aureus*), snake plant (*Sansevieria trifasciata Laurenti*), and a silver-leaved peperomia (*P. hederifolia*).

Of the three, sansevieria, which appears in almost every florist's dish garden, is the most nearly indestructible. It grows slowly and always presents a neat appearance. I have planted it here in a ceramic container with no drainage, as a possible decoration for a mantel piece. I will keep it as long as the plants look decorative, which may be several years, and will then throw them away and replant the container.

Pothos is another accommodating house plant. Individual leaves last as long as two years under good conditions, and it grows so slowly that its form does not change from month to month.

To make the planting in the picture, I put a full three-inch potful of pothos in a low clay pot about four inches across and two inches high; set the pot in the middle of a pewter-washed copper dish; and packed the space between the pot and the edge of the dish with sphagnum moss. Then, as the stems of the plant grew, I trained them clockwise around the pot, holding them in place with hairpins inserted into the sphagnum. Roots formed at each node on the stems and anchored them firmly after the hairpins rusted away.

The planting was two years old when the picture was taken. Two or three times a week I take it into the kitchen and spray it with water from the hose attachment on my sink. This keeps the leaves dust-free and healthy looking. After its bath I tip it on its side to let all the excess water drain away. During the day I keep it on a window sill in my dining room. I use it frequently for a centerpiece at dinner.

In the third dish garden in Figure 32, the black Japanese ceramic vase is worth considerably more to me than the plants. These silver-leaved peperomias cost seventy-five cents each and should be replaced as soon as they begin to lose their decorative looks. If they are given good light and if excess water is tipped out of the vase after each watering to keep the roots from being drowned, they last several months.

POTTED TOPIARY, STANDARDS, AND CASCADES

Topiary, the practice of pruning and training plants into ornamental shapes, goes back to the Romans. It reached a peak in the formal gardens of the seventeenth and early eighteenth centuries, with vast expanses of yew, privet, and box trimmed into geometrical figures or the likenesses of birds, animals, chessmen, and people. Today, topiary is somewhat out of style in gardens but increasingly popular in potted plants. Many flower shows include amateur competitions in eagles or other figures formed of potted ivy, and commercial growers in California regularly offer handsomely clipped plants in pots.

There is no great horticultural difficulty in producing topiary; it demands principally perseverance and a sculptor's eye. The important first step is to select an appropriate plant, preferably an evergreen with small leaves, compact habit of growth, and a propensity for budding freely when pruned. Yews, box, and ivy are the best choices for potted topiary. Other possibilities include ilex, myrtle, eugenia, lantana, chrysanthemum, and small arborvitae.

Clipped topiary

The basic method of producing topiary is clipping, and here the tricky operation is cutting out the original form from an untrained potted boxwood or yew. I would suggest starting with a column, ball, or pyramid, or perhaps an ascending spiral like the tower of Babel. Animals and chessmen are for the expert. Once the form is established, anyone who has ever tended a privet hedge can clip and prune to preserve its outline. Repotting techniques are the same as those described in Chapter Three.

Tied topiary

The ivy eagle in Figure 33 is an example of the second important method of producing topiary—tying to a frame. The first step was

Edmund B. Gilchrist, Jr.

FIG. 33. An American eagle of small-leaved English ivy, *Hedera helix,* trained over a wire frame. Grown by Dorothy S. Keith.

to fashion a three-dimensional frame out of heavy galvanized wire and set it firmly in a pot containing a small-leaved ivy plant with many long branches. Each of these branches was then carefully tied to the frame with light green string, and subsequent growth was fastened in place in the same manner until the frame was completely covered. This tying and training continued over several weeks and involved an unbelievable number of tiny knots. The plant was kept in a greenhouse and rotated slightly every day to avoid having the leaves orient themselves in any one direction. The picture was taken about four months after training began.

Since ivy leaves last only about a year, one or two yellow ones appear almost every day. These are promptly removed with tweezers. In a piece as formal as this, one faded leaf spoils the effect.

As the plant ages, more tying and some clipping will be necessary to keep the bird from becoming overweight. True maturity will find the oldest stems quite woody and permanently set in shape. From this skeleton new growth will continue to appear from adventitious buds and from the small twigs and branches which will have developed along the main stems.

It is also possible to produce topiary by starting with a small plant and tying the branches to the frame as they grow. Frequent pruning of tips will induce the formation of buds and twigs to give thickness to the line of the branch, and well-situated twigs can be allowed to grow into more branches to fill out the shape. This method is much slower, but the tying and training can be done a little at a time rather than all at once.

Standards

The standard shape, a round ball of foliage atop a straight stem, is a stylized version of the natural form of a tree, in contrast to the wholly artificial forms associated with topiary. It can be produced from a wide variety of plants.

The standard in Figure 34 is *Lantana camara* in its second summer. I have grown geranium, heliotrope, abutilon, gardenia, orange, rose, and fuchsia using the same techniques. I start with a

Roche

FIG. 34. Decorative plants on my terrace during the summer. From left to right: dwarf pomegranate (*Punica granatum nana*), tea crab apple (*Malus hupehensis*), Hinoki cypress (*Chamaecyparis obtusa*), spruce (*Picea abies*), mugo pine (*Pinus mugo mughus*), *Lantana camara*, *Begonia multiflora* 'Helene Harms', *Allamanda cathartica Hendersoni*.

rooted cutting which has never been pinched and therefore has a strong central leader. As the plant grows, I remove all side shoots and branches and tie the leader at intervals to a strong stake to keep it from bending or flopping over. I move the plant into a larger pot whenever its roots begin to be crowded, thus keeping it growing vigorously. As a further encouragement to rapid growth, I let all the leaves stay on the main stem until they are ready to fall. The more green tissue the plant exposes to the sun, the more carbohydrates it can make through photosynthesis.

When the main stem reaches the desired height, I cut off the tip and allow side shoots to develop from the top six inches. I pinch these shoots whenever they grow two inches or more, in order to induce as many branching stems and twigs as possible. The result is a full globe of twigs and branches with many buds to develop into blossoms.

When the flowering season arrives, I stop pinching and allow the blooms to form. Lantana and heliotrope benefit from a light pruning of tip growth to renew the foliage and encourage new flowering shoots at least twice during the blooming season.

The question of what is the blooming season is ticklish. All the plants named above bloom best in spring and summer, but you may want them for color at another season. Since none will provide flowers all year round, you must decide when you want them to flower and prune all the branch ends heavily about two months in advance. Lantana produces very satisfactory blooms in winter, but I always save a plant or two for summer flowering because it is a favorite of my hummingbirds.

Standards made from plants with woody stems can be kept for many years. I have seen lantana standards six feet tall with trunks two inches in diameter and said to be eighty-five years old. They are kept to size by pruning of tops and roots as described in Chapters Two and Three. Geranium and heliotrope do not have truly woody stems, and standards of these species are short-lived. They take a year to eighteen months to produce and look well for two or at the most three years, after which you can keep them alive but seldom decorative.

Cascade chrysanthemums

In the fall at some horticultural gardens and a few private estates you may see one of the most spectacular products of the gardener's art—chrysanthemums grown as cascades. Figure 35 shows a cascade grown at Longwood Gardens.

Chrysanthemums are chosen for cascades, not because they are naturally pendant (none are), but because the cascade form displays their masses of bloom more gracefully than their natural upright shape. The so-called "cascade" varieties grow just as stubbornly

G. Hampfler, Longwood Gardens

FIG. 35.   Cascade chrysanthemums displayed in the main conservatory at Longwood Gardens.

upwards as any others; in fact, some gardeners train them on trellises as fans and pillars. They get their name because their long, pliable stems, small leaves, dense branches, and multitudinous flowers make them well suited to training as cascades. Most bloom in late October and early November, with the display lasting three to four weeks, which means they must be given frost protection no later than October 20 in Philadelphia.

Cascades are produced in a single growing season, either from cuttings or from seed. I take my cuttings in December or January from the new basal growth on a plant that has been cut back in the fall and has lain semi-dormant under my greenhouse bench. If I am starting from seed, I sow it in January.

When the seedlings or cuttings are ready for potting, I put them in two and one-half inch pots, where they grow for a month or six weeks. When the main stem is about ten inches tall, usually about March 15, I move the plants into four inch pots and insert a piece of heavy copper wire beside the stem, tie the stem to the wire at intervals and bend the wire to a 45° angle at a point about six inches above the pot.

By this time a number of branches will have developed. I let three or four of these on alternate sides of the main stem grow into additional stems, pinch back all other branches to within one inch of their point of origin, and pinch out all shoots that would otherwise develop into stems. From this point on, each plant will have only the single main stem with three or four parallel stems formed from branches.

As soon as all danger of a hard frost is passed (about April 20 in Philadelphia), I put three plants into a ten or twelve inch pot and settle it outside for the summer. Some of my pots I sink in a flower bed at the top of a wide stone retaining wall, allowing the cascade to extend over the top of the wall, which is level with the surface of the bed. Others I set on a platform about three feet above the ground. It is essential that each plant be allowed plenty of room. If any part of the cascade is crowded by other plants or shaded from the sun for more than an hour a day, the result will be brown leaves and bare places on the stems.

Because of the full foliage produced by the cascades, it is a real problem to keep them from drying out and wilting. Two, or sometimes three, waterings may be needed each day if the pot is exposed to the air. Plants sunk in the ground are easier to keep moist. The lush growth also demands large amounts of fertilizer. I use a water soluble variety and apply it according to the manufacturer's directions, once a week.

When the plants are moved outside, training frames should be substituted for the central wire. Mine consist of a rectangle of wooden slats two feet wide and three to four feet long, depending on how long I want my final cascade, with wide mesh chicken wire tacked across the opening. Hooks are screwed to one end to fit over the rim of the pot and hold the frame firmly in place. If the pot is sunk in a bed, the frame will lie flat on the ground; and in these circumstances you can dispense with the wooden frame and use a length of wire with a hole in it to fit over the pot. If the pot is elevated, the frame will slant downwards from the rim to the ground. The exact angle seems immaterial. When the plants are finally displayed without the supporting frame, the cascade will hang straight downwards in any case.

Some texts recommend that cascades be grown facing south and others that they face north. I have not been able to see any difference between the two exposures. The important thing is to tie the stems to the wire as they develop and to keep all side branches pinched to a uniform length of two or three inches. By the end of August the cascade should present a thick mass of these shoots. On September 1st, pinching is discontinued, and flower buds are allowed to form on the ends of the shoots. Figure 36 shows the kind of training frame used at Longwood Gardens and how the stems are tied to it.

About October 15, with considerable trepidation (sometimes the main stem snaps), I move my cascades into the greenhouse or sunporch, remove the training frame, and set the pots along the edge of the bench or shelf, with the cascades falling over the lip and down to the ground below. The shoots, which grew straight up in the training position, now extend horizontally from the pendant stems, making a thick mat of foliage. The flower buds open in late October and November and continue for several weeks, after which I cut off the stems at the base and store the roots under the greenhouse benches.

Good varieties for training are:

Anna—Single white
Jane Harte—Single yellow
Irene—Double white
Mount Hood—Double white
Desert Sun—Single bronze
White Daphne—Single white

Chrysanthemums are popular in Japan, where they can be grown with very little protection all winter. Kan Yashiroda, in his book *Bonsai: Japanese Miniature Trees,* describes chrysanthemums trained as bonsai, as well as in the form of cascades and modified cascades. They offer many opportunities for gardeners with an interest in decorative horticulture.

G. Hampfler, Longwood Gardens

FIG. 36. A cascade chrysanthemum being trained at Longwood Gardens. Four or five long stems are tied down to the chicken wire frame.

TWO

PRUNING AND SHAPING

The plants we grow as bonsai, if allowed to develop without re-
straint under favorable natural conditions, would be as large as
those we see in the countryside around us. The same is true of many
tropical plants grown in pots. Rubber trees and fiddle-leaved figs
would be as much as forty feet high. Cane-type begonias would be
rangy clumps. African violets would have prostrate stems a foot or
more in length. The ubiquitous philodendron vines would make
their way to the tops of the tallest jungle trees. The challenge of
bonsai growing and pot gardening is to keep these trees, shrubs,
vines, and soft-stemmed herbaceous plants at manageable size and
in pleasing proportions. Basically, this is done by pruning.

PRUNING

Like most of the techniques discussed in this book, pruning is
an art, in the sense that the selection of the branches to be cut and
the decision as to the length of branch to be removed depends on
taste. But the practice of this art must be founded on an understand-
ing of plant growth. Taste points to the end result; horticulture
tells how to achieve it.

Horticultural basis of pruning

To understand the horticultural basis of pruning, you should
know something about the growth of trees, which for this purpose
can be defined as woody plants with single stems. The roots of a
tree serve to anchor it in the ground and to absorb water and dis-
solved nutrients. Its foliage, or more particularly the chlorophyll in

its foliage, uses this water and carbon dioxide from the air to manufacture the carbohydrates which are the basic building blocks of plant tissues—the manufacturing process being called photosynthesis. The trunk of the tree raises the foliage into the sunlight, which is the energy source for photosynthesis, and also transports water, nutrients, and carbohydrates between the roots and the leaves.

As a tree grows, its foliage extends upward and outward and increases greatly in area. At the same time, the trunk and branches grow thicker to support the added weight, and the root system enlarges to provide more water and nutrients. The growth process itself, the actual formation of new cells, occurs only at the tips of twigs and roots, at the buds along the stem and branches, and in the green cambium layer just beneath the bark. The new material is added at the extremities, and in the case of the growth in girth, just inside and outside the cambium layer, without disturbing the inner heartwood.

A young tree must elevate its foliage into the light in order to survive. Thus, for the first year or two, it is apt to consist of a single leafy stem growing straight up. At this stage trees are often called "whips" by nurserymen. Most home owners have bought a whip at one time or another in response to an advertisement in the Sunday paper or from a nursery catalogue. The rubber trees (*Ficus elastica decora*) with single leafy stems sold for house plants are essentially whips, the juvenile stage of a much larger plant.

As the growing tip of a young tree extends upward, leaves appear at intervals along the new growth. These leaves, like all foliage, have a definite life span—one growing season in the case of deciduous trees in a temperate climate, several years in the case of some tropicals. At the end of its life span, the leaf will fall regardless of what care is lavished on it. Dry air, lack of water, too much water, or undue heat or cold may hasten its demise. Intelligent, regular watering; high humidity; and suitable temperature may prolong its life. But sooner or later every fiddle-leaved fig and every rubber tree will lose its lower leaves and look leggy. At this point pruning will usually induce it to branch earlier and oftener than it would in its natural development, thus restoring its attractiveness.

Stimulation of buds by pruning

The explanation for this is in the buds along the stem, which are stimulated by pruning. In the niche (called an axil) where each leaf stalk joins the stem, there is a so-called axillary lateral bud, capable of developing into a branch. At other points along the stem, there are adventitious buds with the same capability; so potentially the tree might develop more branches than there were leaves on the whip. In actuality, only a few of these buds develop into branches. The rest remain dormant as a sort of reserve, in case the developed branches or foliage are lost through attack by insects, breakage in a storm, or other accident.

One of the factors that prevents development of these dormant buds, particularly when the tree is young, is the growing tip at the end of the main stem. Apparently this terminal bud secretes a hormone-like substance which inhibits growth elsewhere. When the terminal bud is pruned away, lateral buds, both axial and adventitious, begin to grow; and the leggy whip becomes a respectable tree. Sometimes this process requires several prunings and considerable time (occasionally a year or more); but if the pruning is repeated often enough, branches will appear. Of all the trees I know, only palms cannot be induced to branch. In that genus removal of the terminal growth usually results in eventual death of the entire stem.

Figure 37 shows a variegated rubber tree (*Ficus elastica doescheri*) which was propagated by air-layering about two years before the picture was taken. About three months before the picture was taken, eighteen inches of the stem, including, of course, the ter-

Edmund B. Gilchrist, Jr.

FIG. 37. Cutting off the top of the variegated fig, *Ficus elastica doescheri*, has induced growth from three dormant buds.

minal bud, was pruned away. A new leader with a new terminal shoot has already grown several inches; the axillary lateral bud below the cut on the right of the picture has developed into a small branch; and if you look closely, you will see that the axillary lateral bud on the left has begun to swell. One more removal of the terminal bud may be necessary before this left lateral branches out in earnest. If all goes well, these new branches will soon transform the plant from a juvenile whip to a mature-looking tree.

Cuts should be made above the buds

The fig in Figure 37 also illustrates another important point. When the terminal bud is pruned, new growth will usually start at a bud close below the cut. This means that the cut should be made just above the height at which you want the branch to appear and at a place where there is a bud to develop—the leaf axil if the leaf is still attached, otherwise the node, the swelling that marks the place where a leaf or a branch previously grew. Cuts made at the axils or nodes will heal readily without dying back. An internodal cut leaves a length of stem or branch which dies back to the next node, forming an unsightly stub.

Once the branches have begun to grow, they in turn can be induced to develop lateral branches by pruning. Removal of the end bud of a branch has the same effect on it that removal of the terminal bud has on the stem. And the same is true of the multiple shoots of woody shrubs. Each of these will branch readily if pruned. A careful thinning out of the shoots followed by pruning of those remaining will change a jumbled clump into an attractive pattern. In fact, it is quite possible to train a shrub into the form of a tree, as shown in Figures 40 and 44.

Results of pruning

Figures 38 and 39 show the results that can be obtained by pruning. In both cases the two plants pictured together are of the same species. The Chinese elm on the right in Figure 38 is a cutting taken from the plant on the left. The two hornbeams in Figure 39

FIG. 38. The dwarfing effect of pruning roots and branches. The plant on the right, *Ulmus parvifolia,* is a cutting from the one on the left.

FIG. 39. The importance of frequent pruning. The hornbeam, *Carpinus japonica,* on the left was pruned about every two weeks during the growing season; the one on the right was pruned only twice in the previous summer at points A and B.

are seedlings, one being two years and the other one year old. Not only does the pruned plant in each pair have more branches and twigs, but they are more irregular and interesting in shape. The reason is that when a branch is pruned, the new bud which is to become the leader starts on the side and not on the end. Even if it finally grows in the same direction as its predecessor, it develops a wiggle in the process. The beginning of this kind of development is to be seen in the new terminal shoot on the rubber plant in Figure 37, which is growing at an angle of about $15°$ from the original trunk. The end result is illustrated in the left-hand hornbeam in Figure 39 and in the zelkova in Figure 8—every irregularity in their branches can be traced to a pruning cut.

Importance of frequent pruning

One further point illustrated by the hornbeams in Figure 39 is the importance of frequent pruning when a tree is growing fast. During the growing season, young shoots extend several inches in a month, and the new wood is relatively straight and of nearly uniform diameter. Examples may be seen in the trunk and main branch on the right-hand tree, which was pruned only twice the summer before the picture was taken, first at point *A* then at point *B*. On the other hand, if the tip is repeatedly pruned away, the wood below each cut is thicker than the new shoot above it, producing the tapered branches in the left-hand tree. A good rule of thumb in dwarfing any tree is to prune before new growth has reached one inch.

Another reason for frequent pruning is to avoid water sprouts or suckers—new, fast-growing upright shoots which develop from adventitious buds when a plant is pruned infrequently and severely. You will often see suckers on old fruit trees that have been drastically pruned to bring them back to proper size. Suckering is said to be caused by shock, meaning the sudden deprivation of a large proportion of the plant's foliage, which stimulates the plant to heroic measures to replace its loss.

Establishing the pattern of the tree

Repeated pruning will produce numerous attractively shaped branches, each of which will bear a clump of foliage when the tree is in leaf. The relative sizes and positions of these foliage clumps and the lines and angles of their supporting branches determine the shape and pattern of the plant. While the pattern can be altered to a remarkable degree by wiring and bracing, techniques perfected by the Japanese bonsaimen and described below, the basic framework is fixed by pruning, by the choice of branches to be retained and those to be cut away, and by the decision as to how long and full each branch is to be.

At this point, the gardener needs a mental image to work toward. One who is artistically inclined may be able to visualize the finished product without assistance. Others will find it helpful to look at specimen trees in a park or arboretum, or wind-blown trees at the seashore and mountains, or to leaf through an illustrated book on trees with an eye for the patterns of nature. Remember, though, that small potted plants cannot be exact replicas of full-grown trees. Their branches must be relatively farther apart to compensate for the proportionately larger size of their foliage. And generally, they are more satisfactory if they have just a few main branches arranged in a simple pattern (see, for instance, the calliandra in Figure 9). The pine in Figure 3 and the zelkova in Figure 8 are outstanding in the degree to which they reproduce the patterns of their natural counterparts. Such results come only with decades of training.

Maintaining the pattern—dwarfing

Once a final pattern has been reached, an achievement that is impossible until the tree is past the juvenile stage, this pattern can be maintained almost indefinitely with little change. Most trees produce leaves only on the current year's growth, the twigs. If the tip of a twig is pruned or pinched after it has grown only a fraction of an inch, a new tip will develop from a lateral bud on the twig itself, but meanwhile the elongation of the branch and the proliferation of leaves will have been stopped. Reducing the number of leaves decreases the plant's capacity for photosynthesis and growth. Thus, repeated pruning and pinching will virtually arrest the overall development of the plant and make it into a dwarf.

A welcome by-product of dwarfing is the decrease in the size of the leaves. Large leaves are associated with vigorous growth and are generally desired in foliage plants because of the luxuriant impression they create. But in potted trees the small leaves associated with slow growth are preferable because they are in better scale with the size of the plant. A striking example of this reduction in leaf size can be seen in the left-hand elm in Figure 38. The effect is also noteworthy in the right-hand plant of the two indoor oaks in Figure 44. Remember, however, that no amount of dwarfing will change the size of a plant's flower or fruit, as the disproportionate plum in Figure 12 well shows.

This dwarfing process, and particularly the reduction in leaf size, can be carried further by removing any full-sized leaves that may develop and by stripping all leaves from a deciduous plant once (or at most twice) during a growing season. All plants form many more leaf buds than normally develop into leaves. It is this reserve supply of buds that enables the trees in our yards to put out a second growth of leaves after the first have been eaten by caterpillars or Japanese beetles. But whether defoliation is caused by insects or by the gardener, the leaves in the second growth are never as large as in the first.

It would not be fair to leave the subject of dwarfing without pointing out that it generally entails sacrificing flowers and fruit on young, fast-growing trees and shrubs. Prunings are too frequent to allow them to develop. This is particularly true of semi-tropical plants that bloom throughout the growing season such as gardenias, pomegranates, oranges, lemons and lantana.

Pruning pines

Our discussion of pruning so far has centered on broad-leaved trees such as maples and oaks. With hardy needle-bearing trees—

FIG. 40. These two specimens of *Serissa foetida variegata,* a tropical shrub, are the same age. The smaller one has been dwarfed by pruning.

pines, spruces, and firs—some modification must be made in the techniques. Pines are perhaps the most different. In the spring the tip of each twig elongates into a light green shoot which resembles, and is called, a candle. Along these candles the needles develop in little protuberances called short-shoots or brachyblasts. If you think of the twig as the handle of a bottle brush and the needles as the bristles, the candle and its needles are like an extension of the brush. At this point the brush consists of two or more (depending on the species) annual crops of needles. In autumn the oldest of these crops falls, so that the foliage is reduced in the winter but not eliminated entirely as in the case of deciduous trees.

The most satisfactory way to prune a pine is to cut the candles just as the embryonic brachyblasts become visible. This has two effects. It reduces the foliage roughly in proportion to the amount of the candle which is removed; if the candle is cut in half year after year, the foliage is likewise cut in half. Also, cutting the candles promotes the formation of new buds at the axils of the short-shoots near the cut; so a pine that has been pruned for several years in this manner will have many twigs and a bushy appearance.

From time to time you may find it desirable to remove some of the twigs in order to thin the foliage and reveal the branches. If so, the best thing to do is to cut off an entire twig. Cutting off part of a twig or cutting a branch between twigs is risky with pines. New buds sometimes develop after a long wait, but more often the twig or branch dies back to the next fork.

To cut the candles of a pine, use small, sharp scissors and cut at an angle between the brachyblasts to avoid harming the needles that will develop from them. The needles of a tree that has been pruned this way several times seem a little smaller than those on natural trees, but the dwarfing effect is not as marked as with deciduous trees. Some authorities suggest shearing the needles themselves to achieve a more dwarfed appearance. In my experience the cut needles have usually developed unsightly brown tips.

Remember with pines that their entire growth for the year is concentrated in the spring production of candles. After the twigs have started to emerge from the candles, additional pruning will not produce additional growth. Also remember with all evergreens that needles once removed will not be replaced. Do not make the mistake of stripping an evergreen as you would a maple or a zelkova.

Pruning other evergreens

Spruces and firs also produce candles and can be treated the same way as pines. However, they bud much more readily than pines, and a cut branch or twig will generally break out with new growth just below the cut. In addition, they tend to develop new buds and needles throughout the summer and are generally more amenable to pruning than pines.

Evergreens with scaly green foliage, like juniper, cryptomeria, arborvitae and chamaecyparis, grow more or less continually throughout the season. Frequent tipping will cause them to bud profusely, producing an attractive, compact appearance. Hemlocks and yews are also improved by frequent tipping.

BRACING, STAYING, AND WIRING

We have seen that pruning will work remarkable changes in the pattern of a plant. And pruning is the safest and most satisfactory way to control its pattern. But there are some effects which pruning cannot produce or can produce only over a very long period—for instance, the twisted trunk of a wind-swept cypress or the drooping branches of an aged hemlock. It is doubtful that pruning alone could ever result in a masterpiece like the five-needle pine in Figure 3. Nature can do it with wind, snow, ice, and the passage of time. If we are to duplicate it, we must use braces to push branches into position, stays to pull them, and wires wrapped spirally around them to hold them in curves or twists.

Bracing

Bracing can be used to spread apart two main stems that are growing in a narrow **Y**, or to depress a branch that is growing like the upper arm of a **K**. A small branch of a shrub will do for a brace. Cut it with a crotch at one end to rest against one of the limbs to be separated. You may be able to find a niche into which the other end can be inserted, but if not, strap it in place with grafting or electrician's tape. The technique of bracing is well illustrated in the dwarf spruce shown in Figure 41. The forked end of the brace straddles the lower limb and is prevented from slipping outward by the base of the small branch. The upper end of the brace is held by grafting tape. The brace is not too close to the crotch of the tree; the greater the distance from the crotch, the less the danger of splitting.

Leave the brace in place nine months to a year, preferably through one growing season and well into the following dormant period. The new growth that forms and hardens in the braced position will resist the tendency of the old wood to return to its original shape.

Staying

Staying is the opposite of bracing. The two stems of a **Y** are bound together to make them parallel; or the upper branch of a **K** is pulled down to the base of the trunk. A stay wire can be seen depressing the lower right-hand branch of the zelkova in Figure 8.

The problem in staying is to keep the wire from cutting into the bark where it is pulled tight against a branch or the trunk. I have used leather or rubber pads under the wire, or loops of plastic tape around the branch or trunk with the wire running between the loops. Another method is to use electrical wire with plastic insulation, leaving the insulation in place where the wire crosses the bark.

Figure 42 shows the kind of situation where bracing or staying is in order. The object is to depress the lower branch as the pointer is doing in the picture, thus giving a more mature and open look to the little tree. This object might be achieved by using a brace like the one in Figure 41. However, the brace would have a tendency to deflect the trunk to the left, which would not be desirable. An alternative would be to run a stay from a point on the branch just below the pointer to a wire around the dish about at the center of the rock. The disadvantage of this course is its tendency to uproot the plant. A third possibility would be to run the stay from the branch to the base of the trunk. This would avoid the uprooting, but would tend to curve the branch inward instead of merely depressing it.

Wiring

If we assume that none of the three methods outlined above is satisfactory, the last resort is to wire the branch itself. Figure 43 shows a box bush where a similar problem was solved by wiring. You can see the wires spiraling up the trunk and out along the limbs. When the wired limb is bent to the desired shape, the wire prevents it from returning to its original position.

FIG. 41. Note the brace used to depress the lower branch of this dwarf spruce tree, *Picea abies breviramea*.

42. Depressing the lower branches s *Serissa foetida variegata* by wiring acing would make it look more e.

FIG. 43. The branches of this *Buxus sempervirens* are held in place by annealed copper wire.

The technique of wiring is described in detail with excellent drawings in *Miniature Trees and Landscapes* by Yoshimura and Halford and is discussed in many other books on bonsai. I list herewith some rules I have found important.

1. Use copper wire. Before use, anneal it by heating it to a fairly high temperature and allowing it to cool gradually. This process relieves the internal stresses in the wire and makes it pliable for the initial spiraling. The bending involved in the spiraling sets up new stresses which make the wire much less pliable once it is wound around the branch. Thus, it is better suited to holding the branch in place. I anneal my wire by cutting it in three-foot lengths, burning excelsior or shredded newspaper over it for ten or fifteen minutes, and allowing it to cool completely before disturbing the ashes or moving the wire.

2. Wire in the fall or the winter and remove the wire in the spring as soon as you see it beginning to cut into the tender new bark. If it cuts through the bark, it will leave permanent scars.

3. When wiring plants with soft bark, such as citrus, gardenia, and most tropicals, wrap the wire first with florist's tape. This reduces the danger of scarring. With pliable trees and shrubs, especially tropicals, you will often find that repeated wirings are needed before the branches will hold their shape. Apparently, wood that grows most of the year stays more resilient than wood that is dormant five or six months.

4. Do not try to wire small, tender twigs and branches. Wait until they become woody. Avoid the temptation of doing any bending, staying or wiring on very young plants.

5. Keep the wiring neat and inconspicuous by winding it in even spirals close to the bark, with secondary wiring parallel to the larger primary wires. Before you try a living tree, practice on a limb cut from a tree or shrub growing in your garden. And study the wiring on any pictures of bonsai you may have. In this book, in addition to the wiring shown in Figure 43, you will see wire wrapped

in florist's tape on the jacaranda in Figure 10 and wire on the hemlock in Figures 45 through 48.

6. When you first try wiring, do not devote all your time to one or two expensive plants, trying to make them perfect. Buy half a dozen cheaper plants and experiment with different shapes and techniques. Try to duplicate the shapes you see in bonsai pictures. Do not worry if some turn out gawky and others die. Artists are accustomed to scrapping a lot of sketches before they get one that is good enough to work into a painting.

7. When it is time to remove the wire, if you have any difficulty unwinding it, use wire cutters to snip it at every twist. It is a pity to break or scar a branch you spent a year in shaping for the sake of saving a length of wire.

For wiring you will need wire of different thicknesses (called gauges), heavy for larger branches and lighter for smaller ones. Different gauges of wire are hard to buy in small quantities, but you will probably find that your electrician has a bin full of scrap wire of every conceivable diameter, which he will just as gladly sell to you as to his scrap dealer. He will also give you hints as to the easiest way to remove insulation. This is important, since all his wire will be insulated. When you are rummaging in his scrap bin, keep an eye open for aluminum wire, which will appear there from time to time. It is valueless for your purpose.

I want to emphasize once more that although the techniques of bracing, staying, and wiring are associated in our minds with bonsai, they are not limited to bonsai. They can be used to improve the appearance of any woody tree or shrub. I know of no better example to illustrate what I said in the introduction, that a short study of bonsai will help anyone who wants to grow decorative plants.

THREE   ROOT PRUNING AND POTTING

Potting a plant properly in a suitable container is essential to a decorative result. The pictures in this book will show you that relatively small containers, either flat and shallow or tall and thin, have a more pleasing look than standard florists' pots. Also, you will see illustrated the basic rules for positioning the plant in its container: put it in the center of round, square, or hexagonal dishes (Figures 1, 4, 11, 49) and about one-third of the way from the end of oblong and oval ones (Figures 8, 10, 43, 48). Finally, you will see that once there is harmony between the plant and its pot, you will want to keep the plant in that pot for a number of months if it is a herbaceous plant or a number of years if it is a woody one. Particularly with expensive oriental containers like the Chinese dish in Figure 8, you will not want to buy a bigger size every time the plant puts on a year's growth.

ROOT PRUNING

You may ask how it is possible to move a tree from a large florist's pot or a nurseryman's burlapped ball to a shallow dish, and how it can be kept in the same dish year after year without becoming potbound and dying. The answer lies in correct pruning of the roots and the top, techniques familiar to any horticulturist but most fully developed by the Japanese. A careful reading of a bonsai text, or better still, a course in bonsai, will give even the most experienced horticulturist new thoughts on potting and root pruning as well as on shaping branches and controlling foliage.

Edmund B. Gilchrist, Jr.

FIG. 44. An extreme example of controlled shape and growth. The two plants, *Nicodemia diversifolia*—the indoor oak, are the same species and age.

Figure 44 is an example of the results to be achieved. The plants are *Nicodemia diversifolia,* commonly called indoor oak and a favorite house plant of mine. They are the same age, having been propagated from the same batch of cuttings about three years before the picture was taken. The large plant is in a six-inch azalea pot. It has never been pruned in any way and has been moved into a larger pot whenever its root system became crowded. The other plant has had its top growth pruned back repeatedly, has been thinned out a number of times, has had stays applied to its branches, and has had its roots pruned twice a year.

When to prune the roots

Most woody plants, of course, will not need root pruning as often as the indoor oak, which has an unusually large, fast-growing root system. For young, vigorous plants, once a year would be nearer the average. Mature plants may go two or more years. In any case, when the roots of either woody or herbaceous plants form a solid mass, so full that there is no loose soil to fall away, the time is at hand for root pruning or a bigger pot. Incidentally, there is only one way to determine whether a plant needs repotting and that is to knock it out of its pot and examine the root ball. Roots growing down through the drainage hole do not necessarily mean the plant is potbound. Often roots will appear here quite soon after repotting. They naturally grow downward in search of water.

When a plant needs repotting, you must decide whether you want a bigger plant, a smaller plant, or one just about the same. If you want it bigger, the best procedure is to put it in the next larger size pot, thus giving the growing root tips new soil to extend into. If you want it the same size or smaller, or if you are going to move it from a deep to a shallow pot or change the shape of its root ball in some other way, you will have to prune its roots before repotting it.

Procedure for pruning roots

I have demonstrated the various steps involved in root pruning and repotting in Figures 45 through 48. The plant in the pictures is a dwarf form of our native hemlock, *Tsuga canadensis,* grown as a bonsai. However, the same root-pruning procedures can be applied to all kinds of potted plants, both woody and herbaceous.

I bought this hemlock from a nursery in Connecticut three years before the picture was taken. It was balled and burlapped and about ten years old. The first fall, I cut back its roots and top rather drastically and put it in a large azalea pot. A year later, I moved it into a deep bonsai pot, again pruning the roots considerably. After a little more than a year in this first bonsai pot, it had

FIG. 45. Root pruning and repotting, step one. The packed root ball shows that this hemlock, *Tsuga canadensis gracilis,* needs root pruning. The moss can be saved and used again.

developed the compact root system shown in Figure 45, and I decided to move it into a smaller pot in better proportion to its branches and foliage. The difference in the size of the pots can be seen in Figure 47, which shows the first pot in the background and the second, smaller one in the foreground. The move was made in winter, when the plant was dormant and no new growth had appeared.

The first step after removing the plant from the pot is to take off the blanket of moss covering the soil, as shown in Figure 45, so you will have it to cover the new soil when you have finished repotting. Moss is sometimes hard to find in winter, the season when most repotting and root pruning is done, and a species that has demonstrated its ability to live in artificial surroundings is difficult to replace. In Figure 46 the moss removed from the near half of the plant can be seen on the potting table at the lower right.

The next step is to remove the plant from the pot and loosen the soil on the periphery of the root mass. A chopstick or heavy knitting needle is a good tool if the plant is small. A hand cultivator is more convenient for large plants and potted trees. As the tool is inserted into the root ball and pried outward, the soil will fall away, and the roots will be exposed and untangled and can be cut off with pruning snips or scissors as shown in Figure 46.

Continue prying loose the soil and cutting the roots until you have removed about one-third of the root ball as shown in Figure 47. This may seem a drastic operation, but it is actually possible to remove an even larger proportion, provided there is a corresponding reduction in the foliage. For example, I have a thirty-year-old American Wonder lemon tree given me by a friend several years ago. It was in a pottery tub two and one-half feet in diameter, a heavy lift for three men. We hoisted the tree out of this monster with a system of pulleys, removed at least half the root ball, cut away the same proportion of the top growth, and worked the plant into a pot that can easily be handled by two people. It is bearing a fine new crop of lemons on my terrace as I write these lines.

POTTING

Choosing a pot

At this point, root pruning is finished and potting begins. The first step in potting is to choose the pot. Once again it is well to keep in mind the bonsai principles, not as hard and fast rules but as guide lines. The most important of these are: make the mass of the pot 20 per cent of the whole and the mass of the plant 80 per cent; use oval or oblong pots for upright plants, tall thin pots

FIG. 46. Root pruning and repotting, step two. The roots have been untangled and about one third of them is being cut away.

FIG. 47. Root pruning and repotting, step three. Root pruning has been completed. The root ball, which formerly filled the larger pot in the background, will now fit into the smaller one, with space for fresh soil.

for cascade plants, and round pots for slanting plants; use unglazed pots for green plants and evergreen trees and glazed pots for flowering plants, harmonizing the color of the pot and the flowers.

To the above I might add that the contrast or harmony in texture between the foliage and the container is an important factor in the result, and that occasionally the shape of the pot contributes greatly to the ornamental appearance. I have a mugho pine, pictured in Figure 49, which is trained in the shape of a low pyramid. It is planted in a flaring Chinese bowl which roughly repeats the shape of the tree, but upside down, giving the over-all effect of a diamond and accentuating the outward spread of the tree.

As for pots to use, the illustrations show that the only boundaries are those of good taste. Increasing numbers of suppliers offer oriental and modern containers made for the purpose. I have found unusual and attractive bowls at ceramic shops and potteries and even at the five-and-ten.

Drilling drainage holes in pots

Any container used for planting must have adequate drainage, at least one half-inch hole for each ten square inches of bottom area. If the container of your choice has no hole, you will find it easy to drill through unglazed pottery with one of the carbide-tipped bits sold for drilling into masonry. Glazed ware is much harder to drill, but patient application of the carbide bit cooled with a little water will finally break the hardened surface. When this happens, if the drill does not move rapidly through the underlying layer, put a prick punch in the indentation and tap it gently. Nine times out of ten a roughly circular hole will break out. If your container is too valuable to risk one chance in ten of cracking, I would suggest taking it to a glass cutter. He uses a soft copper tube as a drill and powdered carborundum as a cutting agent. With this combination and a drill press, he can make a neat hole through glass, which is harder than any glaze.

Now that you have a suitable container, let us return to the

FIG. 48. Root pruning and repotting, step four. Working the new soil into the spaces around the roots with a chopstick. The final touch is to add the moss.

FIG. 49. The triangular shape of the mugo pine, *Pinus mugo*, is complemented by the flaring Chinese bowl. Trained and planted by Yuji Yoshimura.

plant. And here I should say that it is very poor practice to digress this long between root pruning and potting. Bonsai, in particular, should be replanted immediately after root pruning is finished. If for any reason you have to pause, cover the exposed trimmed roots with damp sphagnum or wet paper to prevent their drying out.

Providing drainage

Before putting the plant in the pot, you must provide a way for the water to drain freely out of the bottom holes without permitting it to carry the soil out, too. This is especially important with Chinese and Japanese dishes, which have particularly large drainage holes. The traditional method is to cover the hole with a piece of broken pot, concave side down. If you are using a shallow pot and cannot spare the thickness of a crock, use a piece of burlap or plastic screen to cover the hole.

In shallow pots, where the water must travel more or less horizontally to reach the drainage holes, I generally put a layer of gravel, turkey grits, or coarse perlite on the bottom to provide channels for it to flow through. This is more important in the case of bonsai, where the tree may be in the same container for two years, than in the case of herbaceous plants, which rarely go a full year without repotting.

Setting the plant at the correct height

Above the drainage layer goes a layer of fresh soil thick enough to lift the plant to the desired height. Here again, technique contributes to decorative results. If you look back over the pictures in this book, you will see that almost every bonsai is set with the base of its stem or trunk above the rim of the container and with the top of its ground roots exposed to view. This is particularly evident in Figures 3, 6, 8, 9, 10, and 11.

Exposure of the bottom of the trunk and the ground roots is, of course, a basic bonsai technique, reflecting the Japanese interest in the gnarled roots of ancient, wind-swept specimens. However,

I have found that any plant with a well-defined stem looks better if the junction between the stem and the earth can be plainly seen and if there is an unbroken line from the stem over the edge of the pot, without the harsh barrier of a protruding pot rim. Note the difference between the spruce trees sunken in their training pots in Figure 5 and raised to more or less permanent position in Figure 6. Note also, in Figure 44, the difference between the nicodemia with visible trunk and the one with its trunk hidden by foliage.

Anchoring the plant

Having established the height at which the plant is to be set, you may find it quite top-heavy and insecure, particularly if it was previously planted in the field rather than in a container. In such cases it is important to anchor the plant firmly. No plant will grow satisfactorily if it is wobbly in the soil. Each movement will break off the tiny root hairs through which the plant absorbs water and nutrients and which are the precursors of more roots to come.

Herbaceous plants that are top-heavy or unsteady can usually be supported by tying the main stem to a narrow green bamboo stake. This method of support can be seen in Figure 17. Remember to keep the stake and ties as unobtrusive as possible.

There are at least two ways to anchor woody plants and bonsai. One is to tie the plant in place with string or wire, running three or more stay lines from a crotch in the trunk to an anchor line around the outside of the pot a little below the rim. It sounds difficult, but a little practice will enable you to develop a satisfactory technique. Don't be discouraged with the appearance. No matter how neat your work, the plant will not be decorative so long as the stays remain in place. You should be able to remove them at the end of the first growing season.

The second method of anchoring woody plants is to wire the root ball to the bottom of the pot. If the pot has more than one drainage hole, you can pass a length of wire through two of them and twist the ends together over the main root of the plant, putting a cushion of leather, rubber, or plastic between the wire and the root to prevent cutting into the soft tissue. This is the technique that was used to anchor the large cactus in Figure 24. If there is only one drainage hole, you can wrap the tying wire around a short length of heavy wire as a toggle. In addition to their use as an anchor for the plant, you will find wires through the drainage holes helpful in pulling recalcitrant roots into more desirable positions. As in the case of branches, roots that have been held in place through a growing season will acquire a permanent set.

Bonsaimen differ on the advisability of using copper wire in the root ball. Some feel that because copper can be toxic to plants it should be avoided. Others, including myself, have not noticed adverse effects.

Working new soil around the plant

Once the plant is firmly anchored, fill in more soil around the root ball. In this operation it is vital that all exposed roots be brought into contact with the new soil and that all air pockets be eliminated. Use soil that is dry enough to be easily friable, and work it in around the roots by jabbing it repeatedly with chopsticks, plant stakes, or your fingers, as shown in Figure 48. The old and new soil should be intermingled. Moisture can then move back and forth between them, and the new root hairs induced by the root pruning will be encouraged to grow into the new soil. If you do not do any root pruning on a potbound plant, you may find that the roots do not grow into the new soil. There is no layer of moisture to lure them across the gap from the tight mass of the old to the openness of the new.

Covering the soil with moss

The final step in bonsai potting is to cover the soil with moss. Here, I must leave the reader largely to his own resources, for I have been unable to develop criteria for determining which moss will live and which will die. I go into the woods and collect moss that is growing in a comparatively sunny spot and that looks attractive. I place this on the surface of the soil, being careful to press the edges of the moss clumps close to one another, so that there is no gap between the pieces for water to run into and enlarge. When the surface is completely covered, I soak the pot in water up to its rim for five or ten minutes and settle the moss firmly into the moist earth with my fingers to establish a contact across which moisture can move. In most cases, the moss soon takes root and flourishes, at least initially. Sometimes moss will last a year or more. Sometimes it proves unable to withstand artificial conditions and withers in a few weeks. When it needs replacing, you have a good excuse for a pleasant walk in the country. Keep your eye open for blue-green lichens. Many of these grow surprisingly well on potted plants, and they add a great deal to the appearance of bonsai and similar plantings. Occasionally you will find a small piece of rotten wood covered with moss or lichens, which can be half-buried in the soil of your planting. Such a piece can be seen in the right foreground of the group planting of *Acer ginnala* in Figure 28.

Final words of caution

These final words of caution are in order. First, do not prune or in any way disturb the roots of a dwarfed woody plant from midspring to midsummer, the time of active growth. During this period the plant needs every drop of water its roots can provide to sustain its active growth processes. The inevitable dislocation and breakage of root hairs in the root-pruning and subsequent repotting process curtails the intake of water and may easily cause desiccation and death.

Second, whenever you prune the roots of any actively growing plant, make a corresponding cut in the foliage. A healthy plant achieves a balance between the root surface, which absorbs water, and the leaf surface, which transpires it. When a plant's root system is constricted by a pot, this balance tends to be heavy on the side of foliage. The transpiring leaf surface is, if anything, too large for the absorbing root surface. This is one reason why luxuriantly growing potted plants wilt easily and why periodic pruning of all potted plants is a good idea. If you take a plant that is already overbalanced on the side of foliage and prune away a substantial portion of its roots, you will tip the scales too far. Again, desiccation and death may result.

Finally, keep newly root-pruned plants in the shade to allow new root hairs to form and make contact with the soil before photosynthesis and transpiration begin in earnest. The length of time will depend on the environment, the season, and the plant, but should never be less than a week.

FOUR

WATERING, SOILS, FERTILIZING AND PEST CONTROL

The basic factors in the culture of potted plants are light, humidity, temperature, water, soil, fertilizer and pest control. I discussed them all in detail in my earlier book, *Garden in Your House,* and since I view this book in some ways as a supplement to that one, I will not repeat or summarize that discussion here. I will merely add a few thoughts that seem especially pertinent to bonsai and decorative plants. Therefore, the following pages are not a complete manual of culture. Any of my readers without experience in growing plants in pots should study *Garden in Your House* or one of the many other texts on the subject.

WATERING

I am often asked how frequently bonsai and house plants should be watered. There is, of course, no easy answer except to say that no potted plant which is not a native of the desert should ever become dry. Equally important, no plant should ever be left sitting in water after the root ball is saturated. The persons who have most success with potted plants, indoors and out, are those who are always aware of the weather. They know without thinking whether the humidity is high or low, whether or not the wind is blowing, and whether it is sunny or cloudy. They can predict about when their plants will need watering, and they put the needs of their plants first. On a sunny summer day when the air is dry and the wind is blowing, some plants will need water two or even three times. During humid overcast spells, some plants may need attention as seldom as once a week. Observation is the key, and your hand is the best gauge to determine the need. I touch the moss-covered root balls of many of my plants once or twice every day to feel how dry they are.

Plants in shallow pots with full foliage will dry out far faster than plants in deep pots. Bonsai, which are apt to have a disproportionately small root system, will dry out in a matter of hours in hot, sunny weather. Syringing the foliage will cut down the rate of transpiration considerably and should be done at least once a day during the growing season if the air is dry.

Extra care is needed in watering mounded bonsai like those in Figures 1 and 9 because of the tendency of the water to run off the elevated soil if the moss is dry. When I have such plants in the house, I wet the moss with a hand sprayer a minute or two before watering and find that the damp moss then absorbs water quite readily. Outdoors or in the greenhouse, I use either a flaring rose nozzle or a fog nozzle on the hose to wet the moss and water the plant at the same time. If you water by hand, make it a point to soak small plants about twice a week by immersing them, pot and all, in a basin of water until they stop bubbling.

Vacation, holidays, and work days

Watering presents a very real problem for bonsai fanciers taking a vacation. Hardy bonsai can be left without watering for a week or more in winter if they are in a suitable pit, but I have no tricks to recommend for safely leaving them over summer week ends or holidays. In Japan, and I imagine on the west coast of the United States, amateurs can board their plants at a bonsai nursery when they are away from home. Perhaps you can make a similar arrangement with a local nurseryman or find a reliable friend to take care of your plants for you. If not, and you are a frequent week-ender, this type of plant is not for you.

During spring and summer I grow most of my bonsai and woody plants in locations which are sunny for six to seven hours a day.

This, coupled with frequent light fertilizing, encourages healthy, compact growth over a long period; but it also necessitates more frequent attention to the moisture content of the soil in the pots than would be required if the plants were growing in semishade. If you have to leave your collection all day long during the growing season, you will have to put them in a fairly shady place.

House plants are in some ways the opposite of bonsai in regard to vacations. They will go up to a week without being watered in the summer if they are dug into a shaded bed. But in winter they need attention every day. Again, boarding greenhouses or horticultural sitters are the ultimate answer.

SOILS

Potted plants are watered two or three hundred times a year. This fact determines the kind of soil to be used. The frequent watering and the expansion of growing roots within the confines of the pot pack most potting soils into a tight mass which becomes less and less pervious to water. To counteract this tendency, I use a high percentage of organic matter—peat moss, leafmold, and the like—in the growing medium. Its resiliency resists the packing effect of watering and root growth. Also, this spongy material retains a large proportion of water, distributes it uniformly throughout the root ball, and provides numerous tiny spaces for air to circulate as well as water.

Soil mixtures

In making a potting mixture, I start with compost. To this I add peat moss to give the soil a spongy structure and to increase its water-holding capacity. Then I add rather large amounts of sand or perlite to promote drainage and also to induce the roots to twist and turn.

I have confirmed the beneficial effect of sand and perlite on root growth by observing my own plants. When sand or perlite is omitted from the mixture, I find that the roots grow straight out and down until they meet the solid walls of the pot and then twist and turn, looking for more fresh soil. In contrast, plants that I grow in a compost and peat mixture with the addition of sand or perlite show more root growth in the soil close to the trunk. When the tip of a root hair impinges on a sand particle, the hair changes its direction of growth and starts off at a relatively sharp angle until it hits another particle and changes course again. The result of this zigzagging is a mass of roots throughout the pot and not just at the edges.

Here is a suggested soil mixture for bonsai and other potted plants:

> 3 parts compost
> 2 parts sphagnum peat moss
> 1 part coarse builder's sand or coarse perlite

These ingredients should be available to every gardener. The compost I collect in my garden, the peat moss and perlite I buy at a garden supply center, and the sand comes from our local coal yard. A discussion of their functions in the soil appears in *Garden in Your House*.

Acidity not a problem

I worry little about the acidity of the soil. The large proportion of peat moss in all my soil mixtures results in a mildly acid reaction (pH 5.8 to 6.5) which varies little from one batch to another because peat moss is an excellent "buffer" and resists changes in acidity. The great majority of plants grown in pots are accustomed to about this same acidity in their natural growing medium.

Sterilizing the soil

Any soil used in pot gardening should be sterilized, or more properly, pasteurized, either with chemicals or by heat. Sterilization is standard practice with commercial growers, and amateurs will be surprised at how it will improve their over-all results and reduce the incidence of root rot, crown rot, nematodes, damping-off, and other pests and diseases. My method is to fill a fifty-gallon drum with mixed soil, adding an ounce of tear gas (chlorpicrin, sold under the name "Larvacide") at the quarter, half, and three-quarter stages, and sealing the top with a sheet of plastic. Forty-eight hours later the soil can be dumped from the barrel. It will be ready for use as soon as the gas dissipates, a process which takes a few minutes if the soil is agitated and several hours if it lies undisturbed. The sterilized soil is entirely free of pathogens. The brochure accompanying the tear gas says that it will not be effective at temperatures below 70° F.

If the tear gas treatment is too cumbersome or too frightening, you can sterilize small batches of soil by cooking them for two hours in a 200° F. oven. Other effective sterilizing agents are formaldehyde and two proprietary chemicals sold under the names "Mylone" and "Vapam."

FERTILIZING

For fertilizing I use a water-soluble chemical fertilizer with a high proportion of nitrogen, manufactured especially for potted plants. A number of formulations are available under various trade names. Because they are soluble, they can be absorbed immediately by the roots of the plants, and by the same token, what the plant does not take up is soon washed out of the soil.

I use this type of fertilizer once a week from January to October on all young, fast-growing, flowering, and fruiting plants, mixing it at about half the strength recommended on the can or bottle. I fertilize older, slower-growing plants every two weeks, still at half-strength. Never fertilize a plant that is sickly, wilted, or dormant.

Those who have read traditional texts on bonsai may wonder why I recommend soluble fertilizers, which are inorganic, instead of the organic substances—rape seed, cottonseed, fish meal and manures—which the Japanese have used for centuries. The reason is simply that modern inorganics are more reliable. The Japanese used organics because they were the best, and indeed the only, fertilizers obtainable. But their action depends on the proper micro-organisms living in the proper combination of temperature, moisture and acidity. If any link in the chain is broken, as it often is in pot culture, the nutrients in organic materials do not become soluble and available to the plant. By contrast, inorganics are independent of bacterial action. They are immediately soluble and available.

INSECT CONTROL

The insects that are most likely to be troublesome on bonsai and other potted plants are mealy bugs, scale, aphids, spider mites (not actually insects), and Japanese beetles. Push-button insecticide bombs are sold in most hardware and garden supply stores. Their labels state clearly what insects they will control. They should be used regularly to prevent infestation as well as to eliminate marauders already present.

If your collection is large, you may find it more practical to make up a spray mixture every ten days or so. You should include an insecticide for sucking insects (nicotine sulfate, malathion or "Sevin"); a miticide ("Dimite," "Aramite," or "Kelthane"); and, in summer, a stomach poison for caterpillars and beetles (arsenate of lead or "Sevin").

Do not neglect this cultural chore. Nothing is less decorative than a plant that has fallen prey to attack.

INDEX

Abies, 21, 98
Abutilon: grown as standard, 81; megapotamicum, 52
Acacia Baileyana, 40
Acer, 21; buergianum, 28; campestre, 28; ginnala 28, 67, 72; seedlings, 69
Acidity of soil, see Soils
Adiantum, 57
Aechmea 'Foster's Favorite,' 66
Aeschynanthus, 52
African Violet, see Saintpaulia
Agave, 60
Aglomorphia coronans, 65
Anthurium, 64
Apple, see Malus
Apricot, see Prunus
Arborvitae, see Thuya
Asparagus Sprengeri (asparagus fern), 52
Asplenium nidus (birds nest fern), 65
Azalea, see Rhododendron

Bamboo, 27
Bauhinia, 40
Beech, see Fagus
Begonia, 52; bartonea 'Winter Jewel,' 44; venosa, 46
Betula alba, 28
Billbergia: Leitzei. 65–67; Saundersi, 65, 66, 67
Birch, see Betula
Bonsai: derivation of word, 13; hardy bonsai, 13–30; care, 14–18, 19, 20; display, 12, 18; fertilizing, see Fertilizing; history, 13; plant list, 28; watering, 15, 17, 19, see also Watering; importation, 20, 21; Mame bonsai, 37, 38; miniature bonsai, same as Mame bonsai; natural bonsai, 22; collection techniques, 23; shaping bonsai, see Pruning, Wiring; tropical bonsai, 30–42; care and display, 31; plant list, 40
Boston Fern, see Nephrolepis

Box, see Buxus
Bracing, see Shaping
Bromeliads, see under following generic names: Aechmea, Billbergia, Tillandsia, see also Driftwood Plantings
Browallia speciosa major, 52
Buds, 90, 98
Burro Tail, see Sedum morganianum
Buxus, 28, 80; microphylla

Cacti: care and culture, 60; Lemaireocereus, 59; pruning, 61; sunburn, 60; see also Desert plants
California Pepper Tree, see Schinus Molle
Calliandra surinamensis, 32, 40, 69
Calluna vulgaris, 29
Camellia: japonica, 40; sasanqua, 41
Carissa grandiflora, 37, 41
Carpinus: caroliniana, 29; japonica, 29
Cascade chrysanthemums, 83–87; plant list, 87; technique, 85
Cassia eremophila, 41
Cedrus: atlantica, 29; deodara, 29
Chaenomeles japonica, 29
Chamaecyparis, 29, 82; obtusa, 7, 20
Cherry, see Prunus
Chinaberry, see Melia Azedarach
Chlorophytum, 52
Chrysanthemums, 80; as bonsai, 87; see also Cascade Chrysanthemums
Citrus, 30, 36, 41; calamondin, 41; kumquat, 41; lemon, 41, 108; lime, 41; orange, 81; tangerine, 41
Classic myrtle, see Myrtus
Climbing fern, see Lygodium
Cold frames as bonsai shelter, 17, 20
Columnea, 52
Containers, 37, 44, 104, 108–109; concrete, homemade, 71; drainage holes, drilling, 32,

110; drainless, see Dish gardens; driftwood, 62–68; proportion to plant, 44, 108; rocks, 72–76; see also Potting and, as to containers shown in pictures, text describing plant in picture
Cotoneaster, 29, 38
Crabapple, see Malus
Crataegus: oxyacantha, 29; phaenopyrum, 29
Cryptomeria japonica, 29
Cuphea hyssopifolia, 41
Cupressus: arizonica, 41; macrocarpa, 41
Cypress, see Cupressus

Davallia, 52, 65; griffithiana, 63, 65
Delonix regia, 41
Desert plants, 60–62; see also Cacti, Succulents
Dish gardens, 78–79; drainless containers, 77, 79; general discussion, 68; repotting, 76; rock plantings, 74; seedlings, 69; succulents, 61; see also Containers, Group plantings
Dormancy: essential to spring foliage and bloom, 16–17; safest time to repot and root prune, 115
Drainage: essential in potting, 112; holes: covering, see Potting; drilling, see Containers
Driftwood plantings, 62–68; bromeliads, 65, 66, 67; fastening driftwood in container, 60; ferns, 64; hold fast roots, 63; osmunda fibre, 62; technique, 62; wood preservative, 64
Dwarf species, 28
Dwarfing, see Pruning

Echeveria derenbergi, 61, 62
Elm, see Ulmus
Epiphytes, 62, 64, 65; planting in driftwood, 63, 64; fertilizing, 64
Episcia, 52
Eugenia uniflora, 41, 80
Euonymus, 21, 29
Euphorbia, 60

123